BLACK

INVENTORS

Coloring Book

Adult Coloring Books

Aryla Publishing 2018

978-1-912675-30-2

www.arylapublishing.com

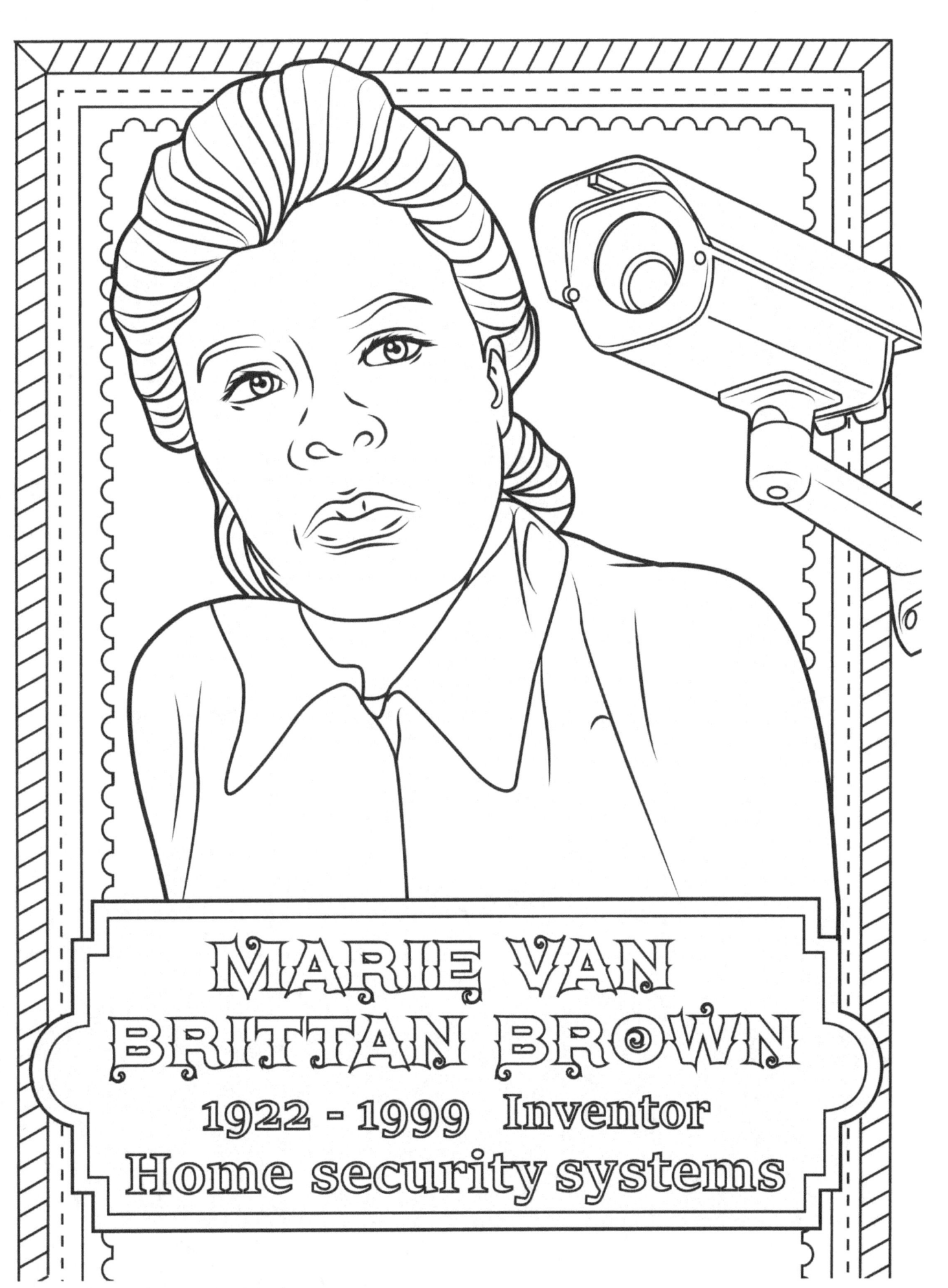

MARIE VAN BRITTAN BROWN

1922 - 1999   Inventor

Home security systems

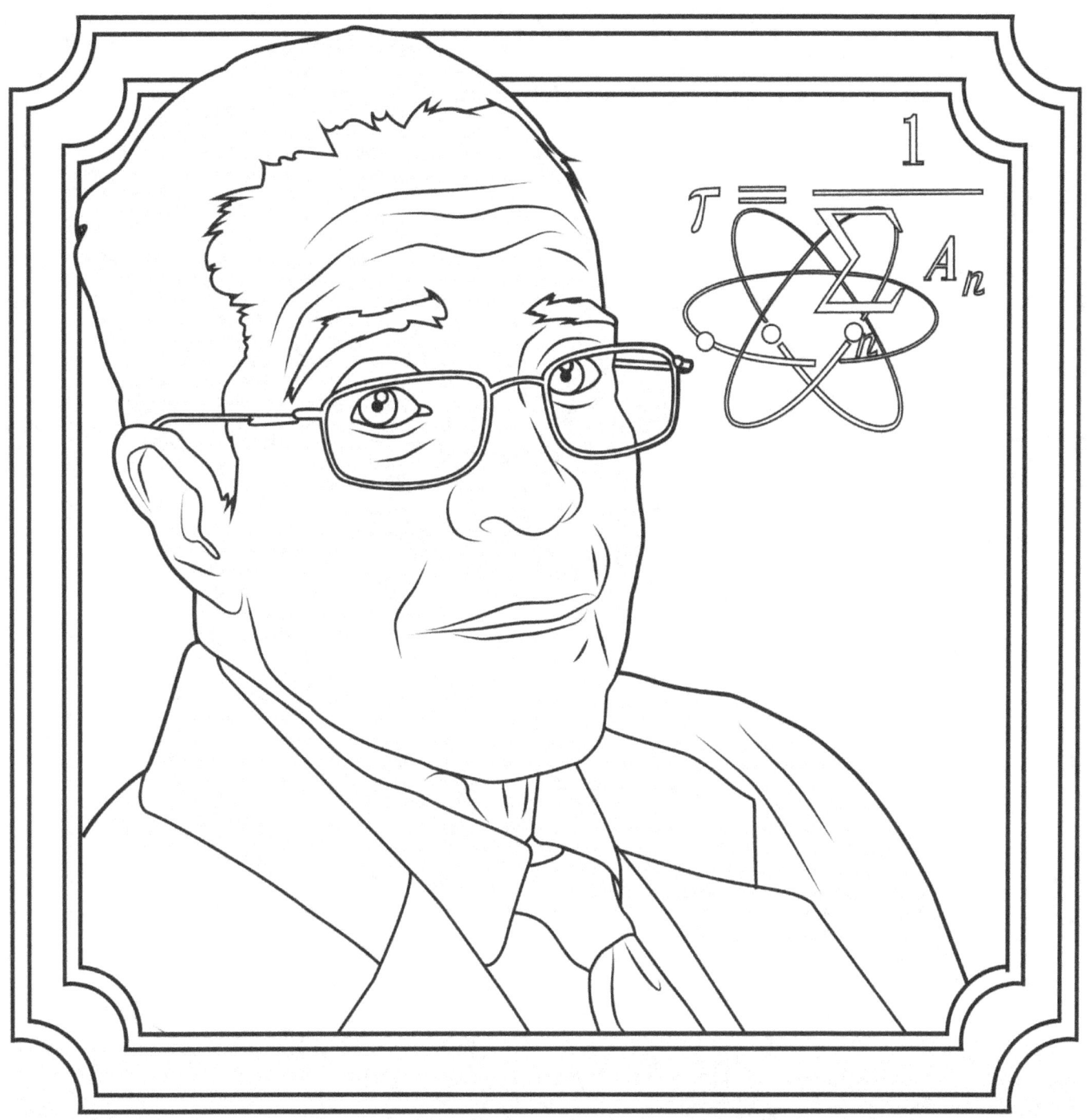

Jesse Ernest Wilkins Jr
1923 - 2011 - Mathematician

Mathematical models to explain gamma radiation

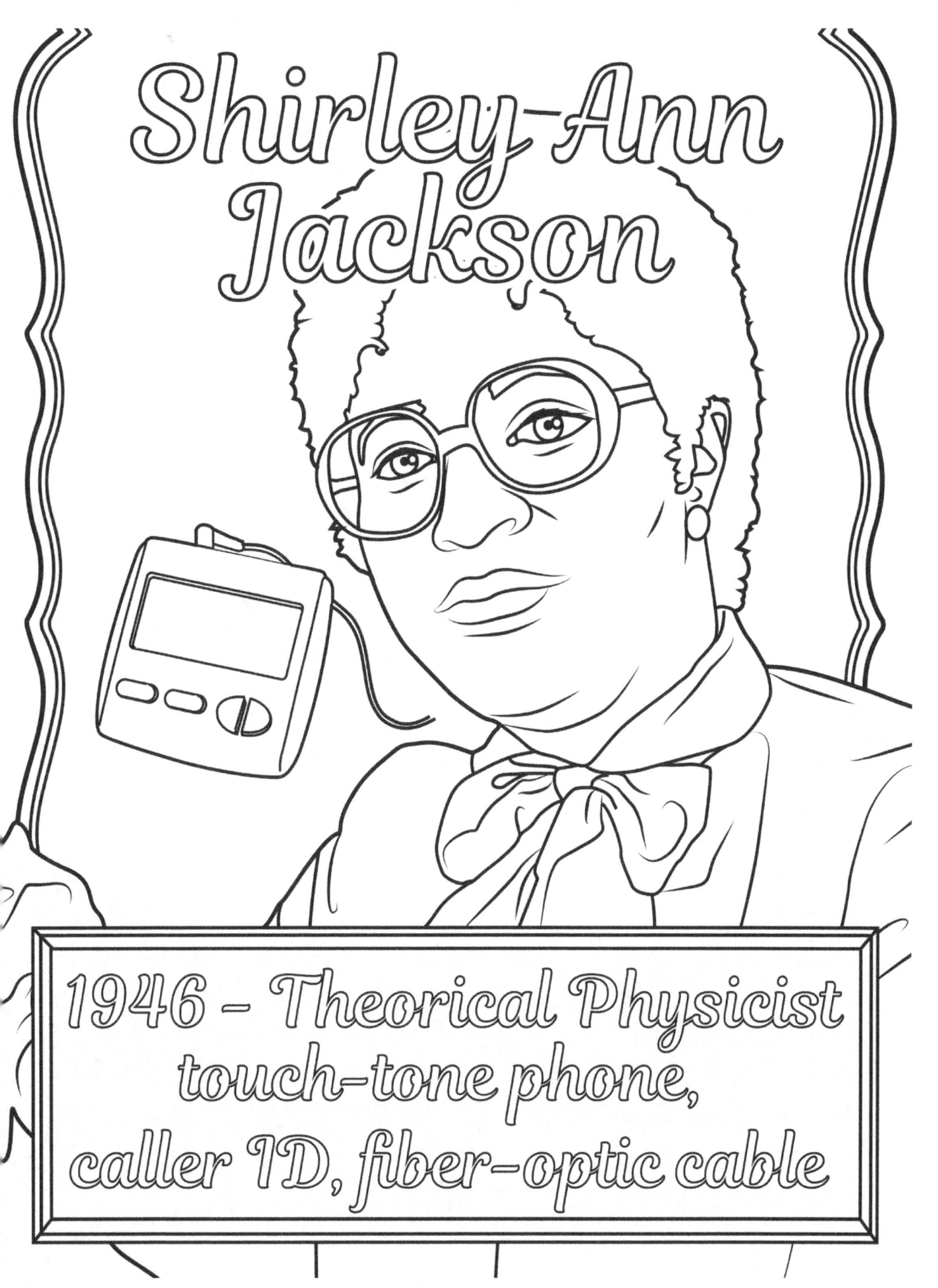

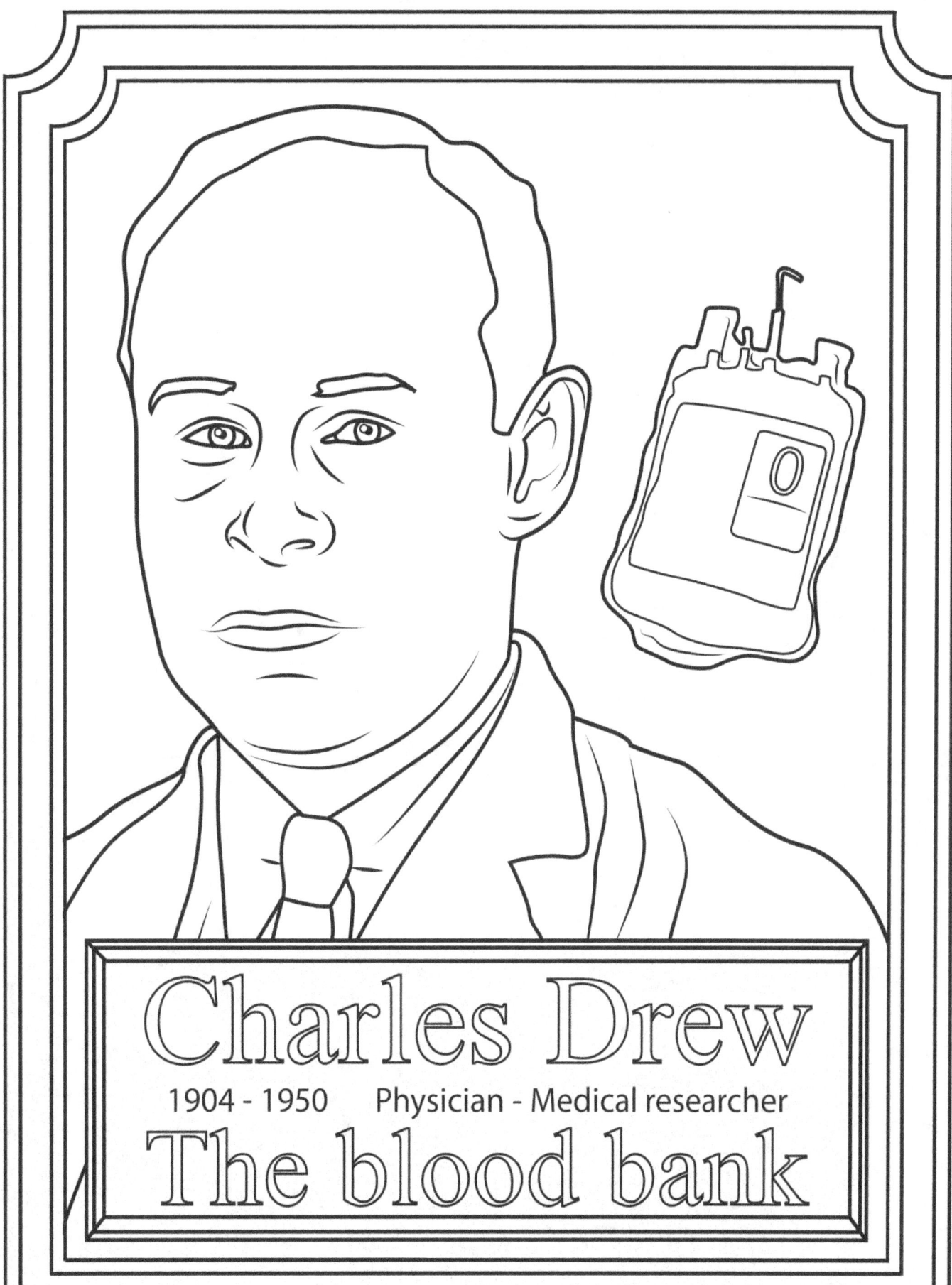

Charles Drew

1904 - 1950   Physician - Medical researcher

The blood bank

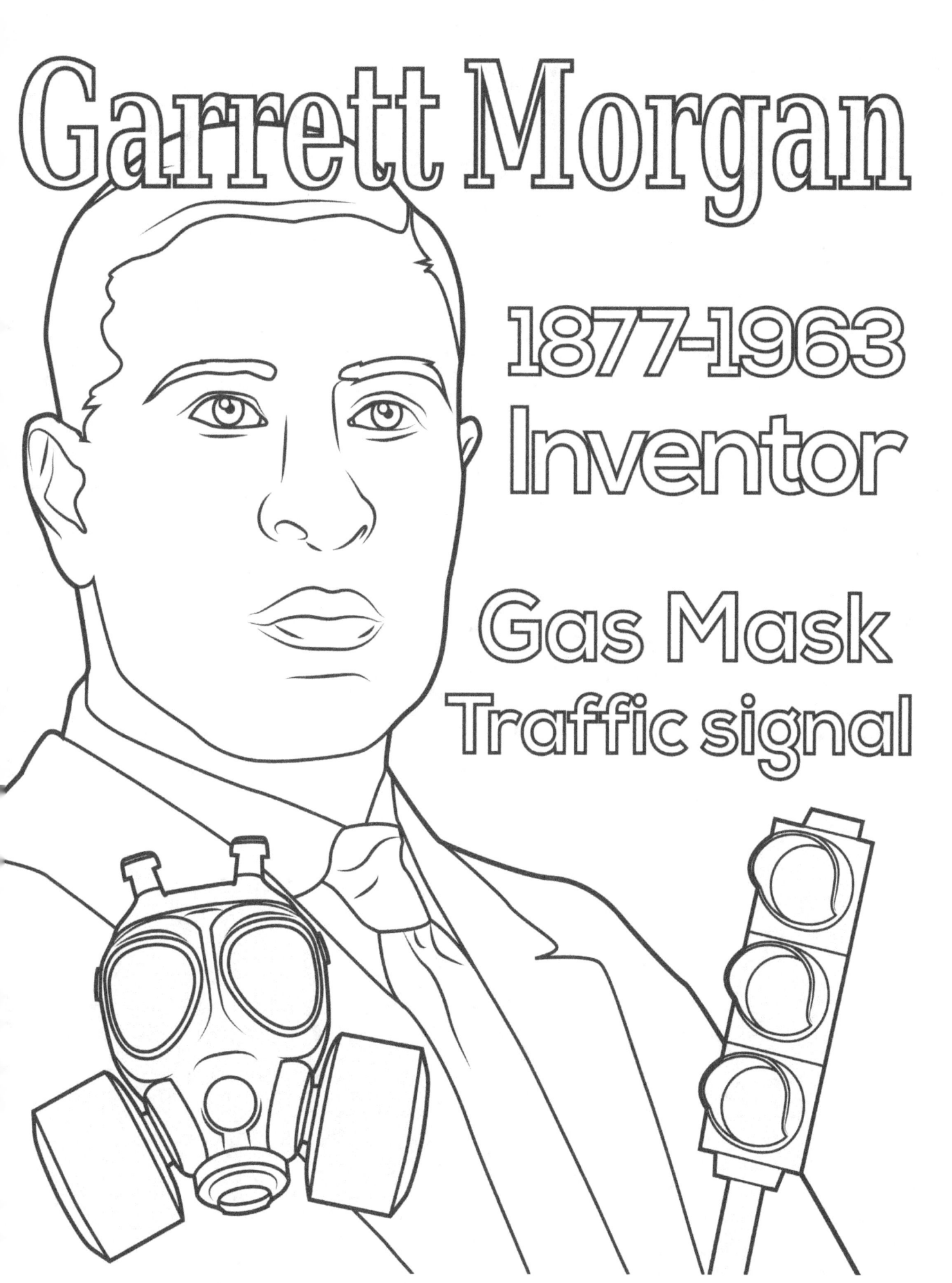

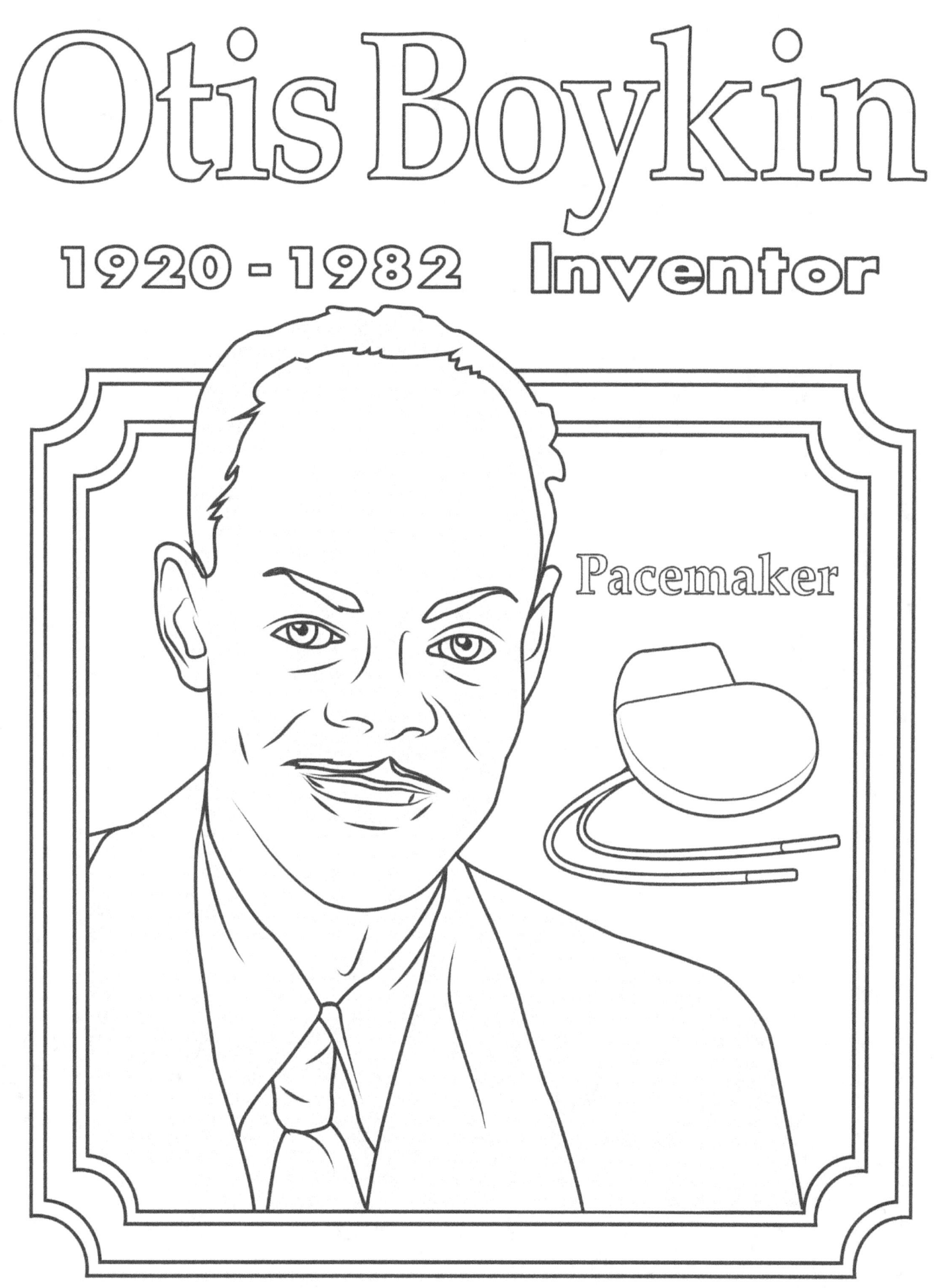

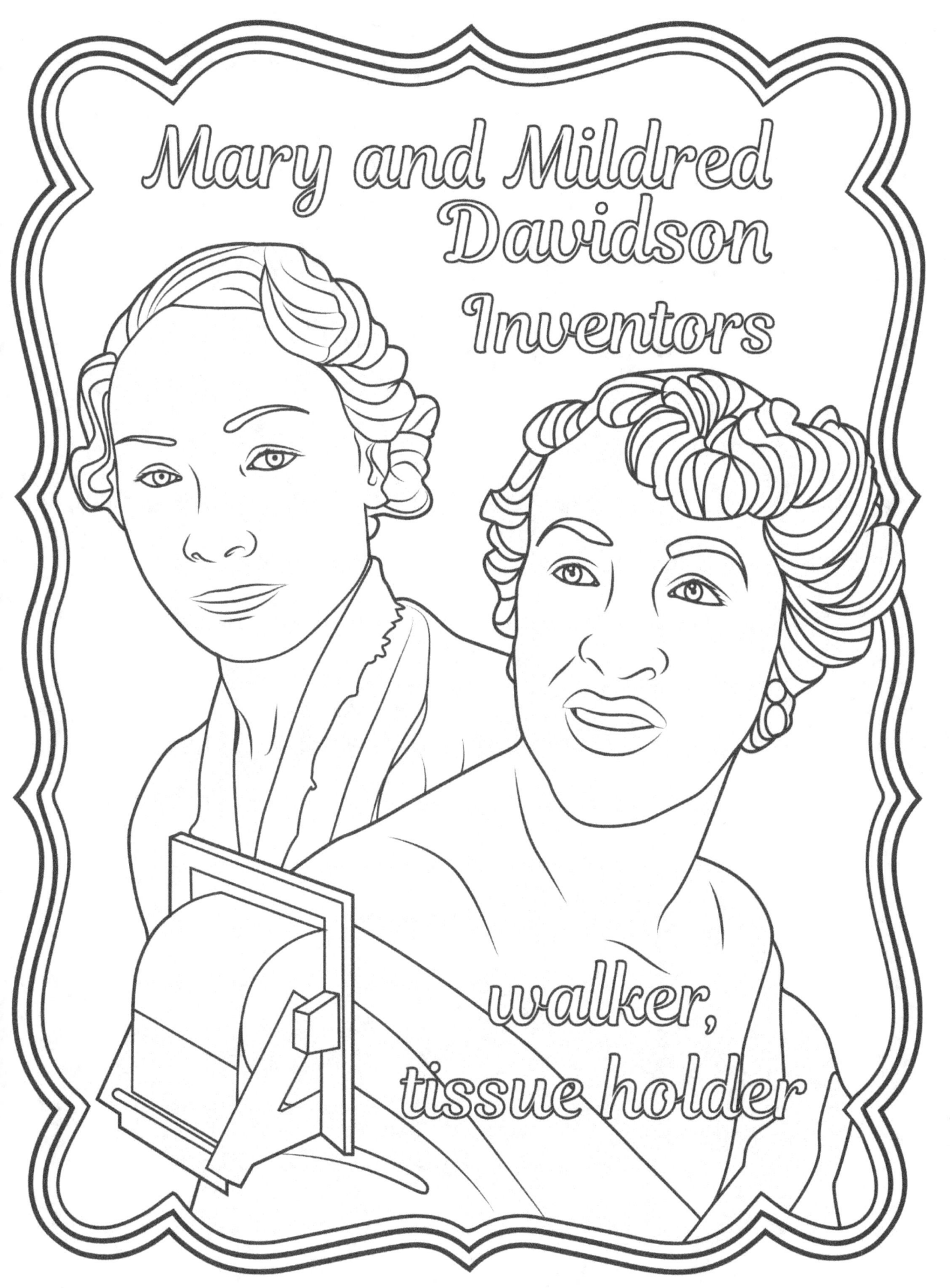

Mary and Mildred Davidson

Inventors

walker, tissue holder

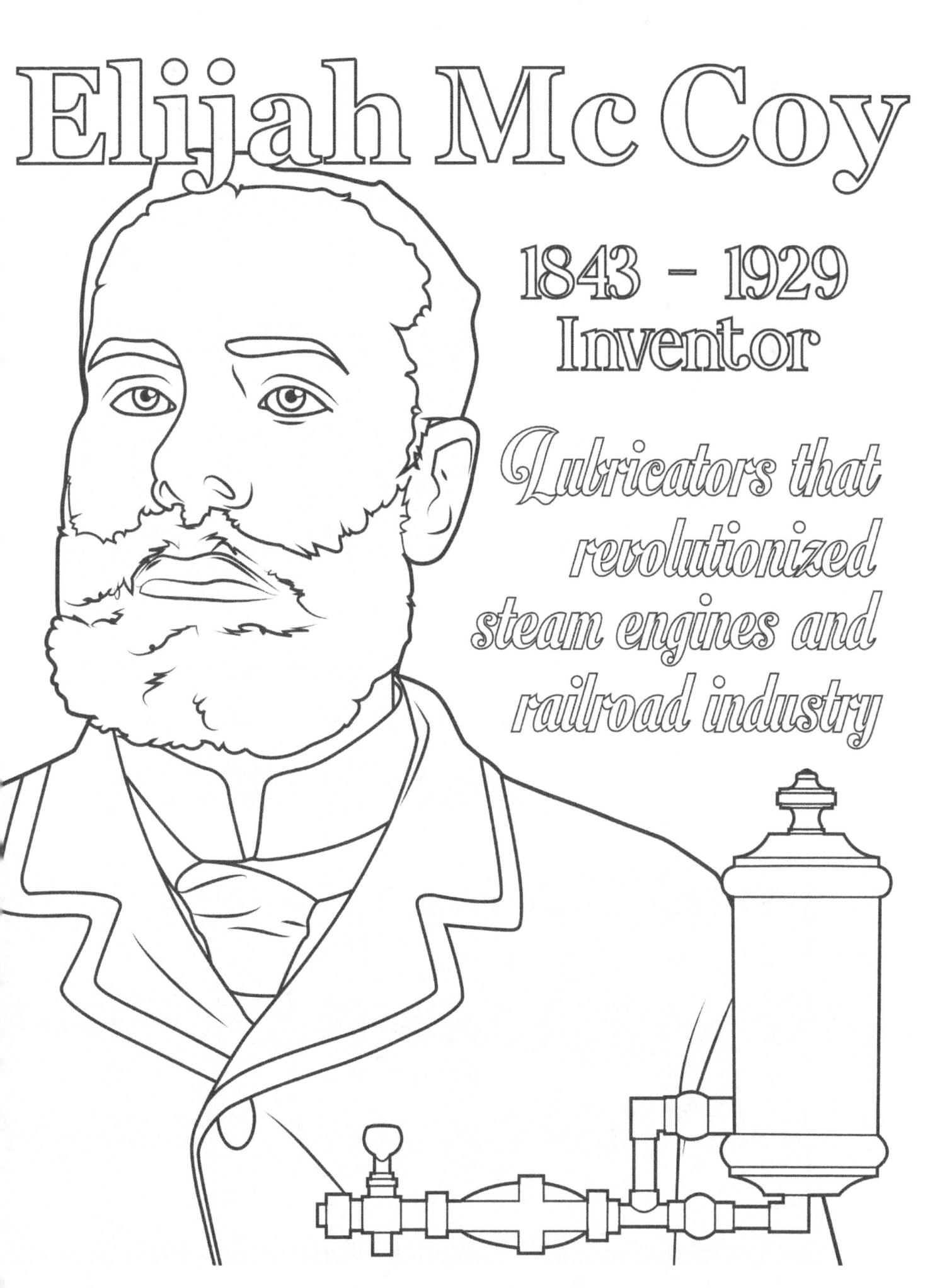

Elijah McCoy

1843 – 1929
Inventor

Lubricators that revolutionized steam engines and railroad industry

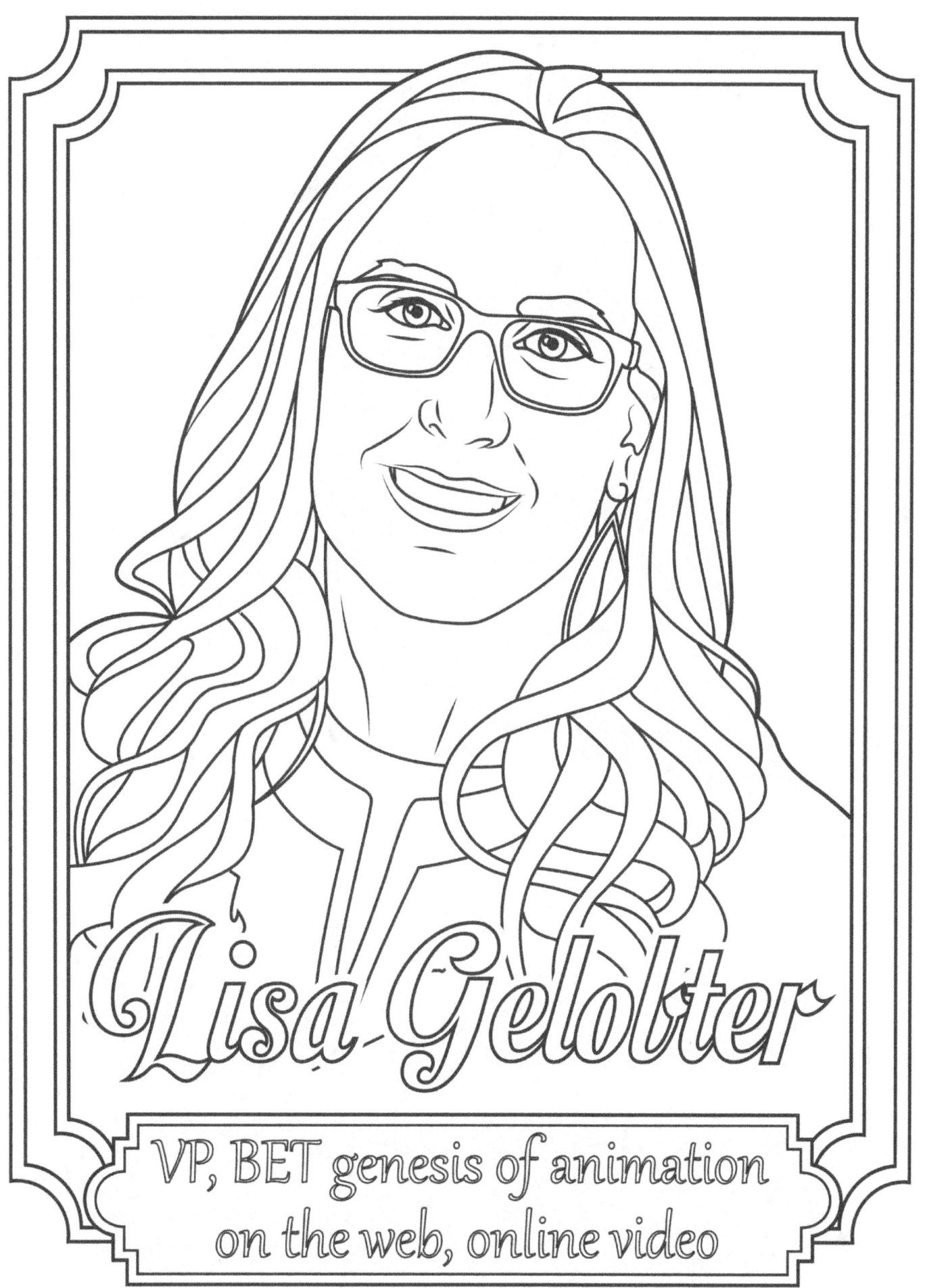

Lisa Gelobter

VP, BET genesis of animation
on the web, online video

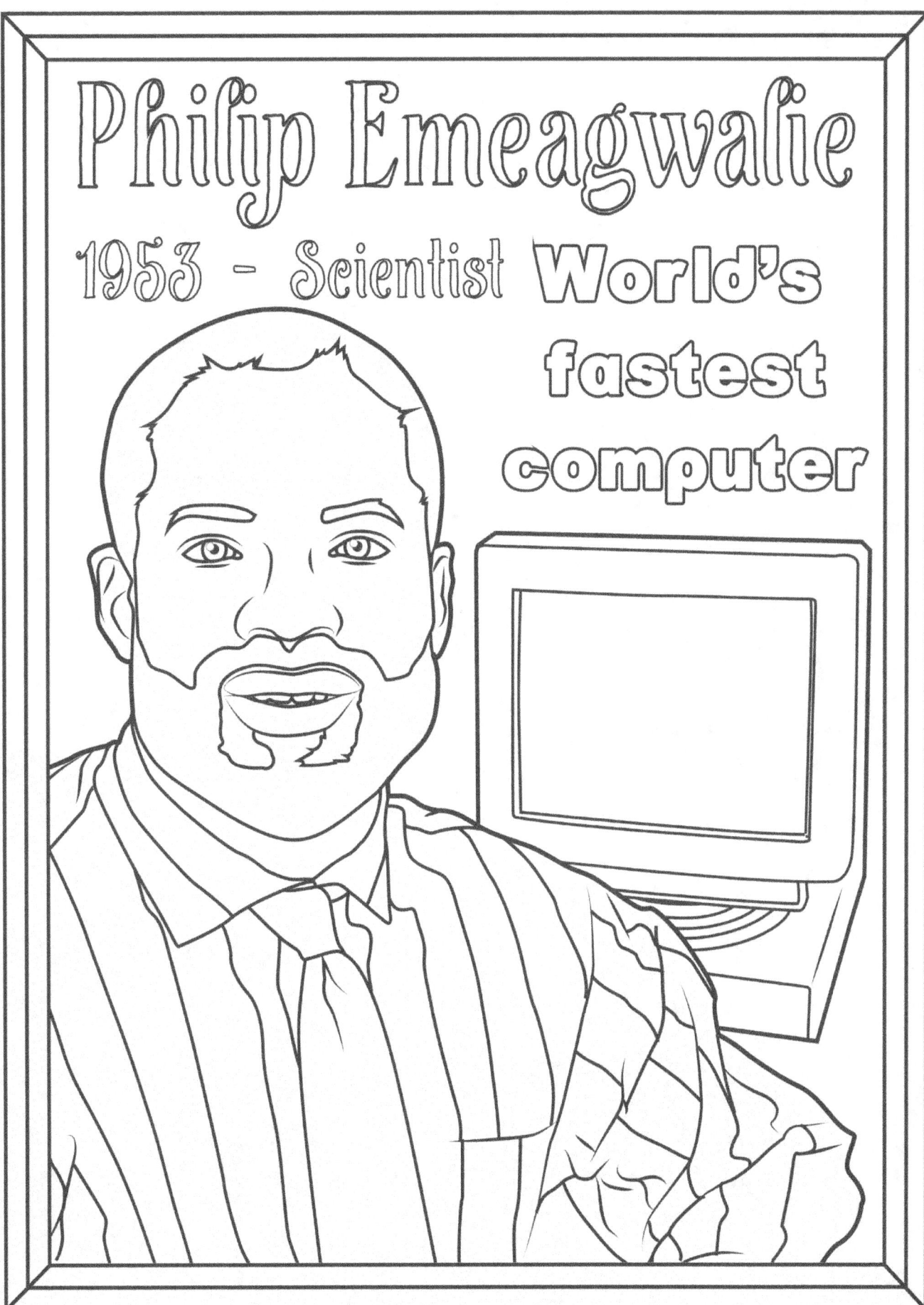

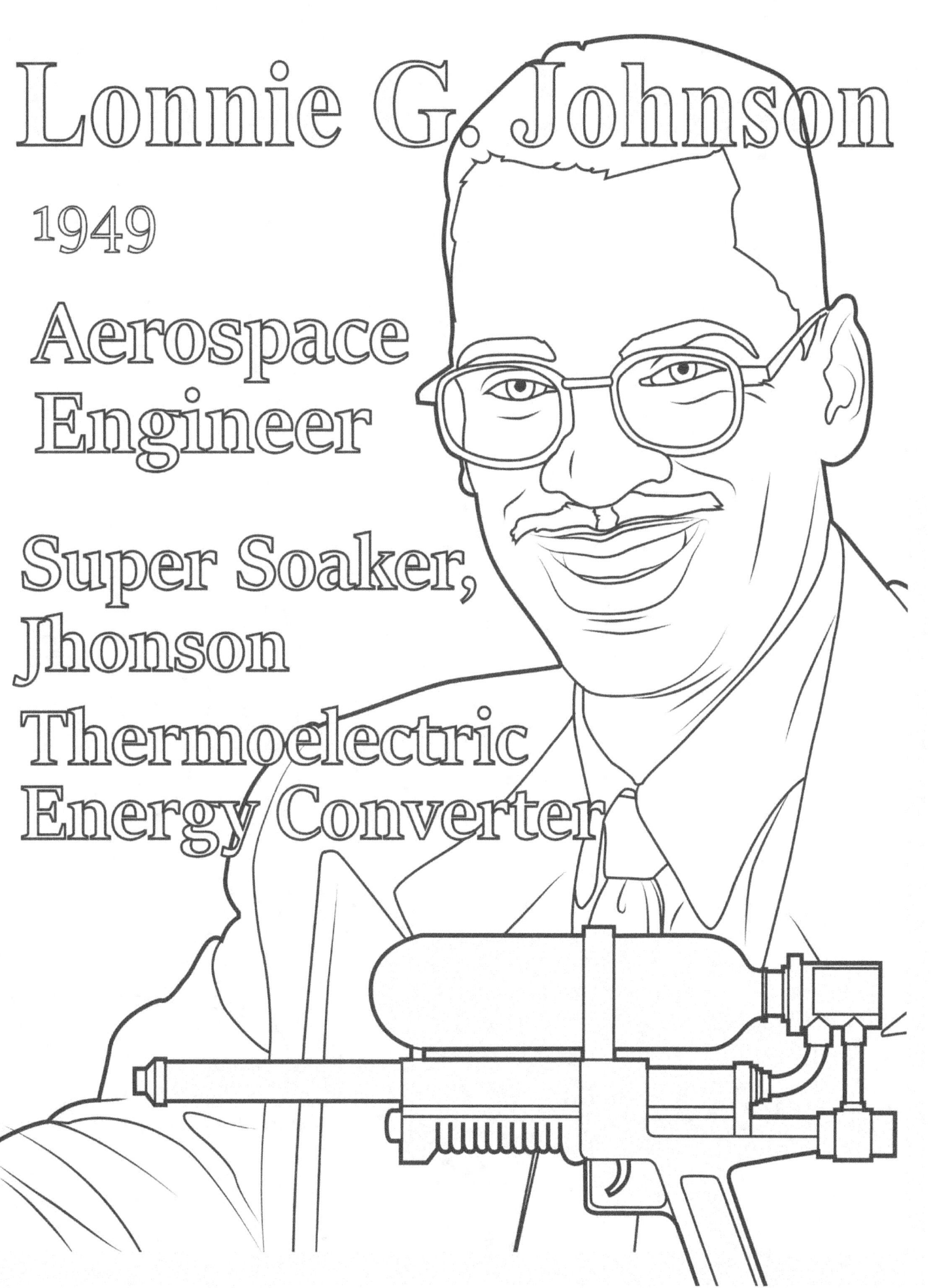

Lonnie G. Johnson

1949

Aerospace Engineer

Super Soaker, Jhonson Thermoelectric Energy Converter

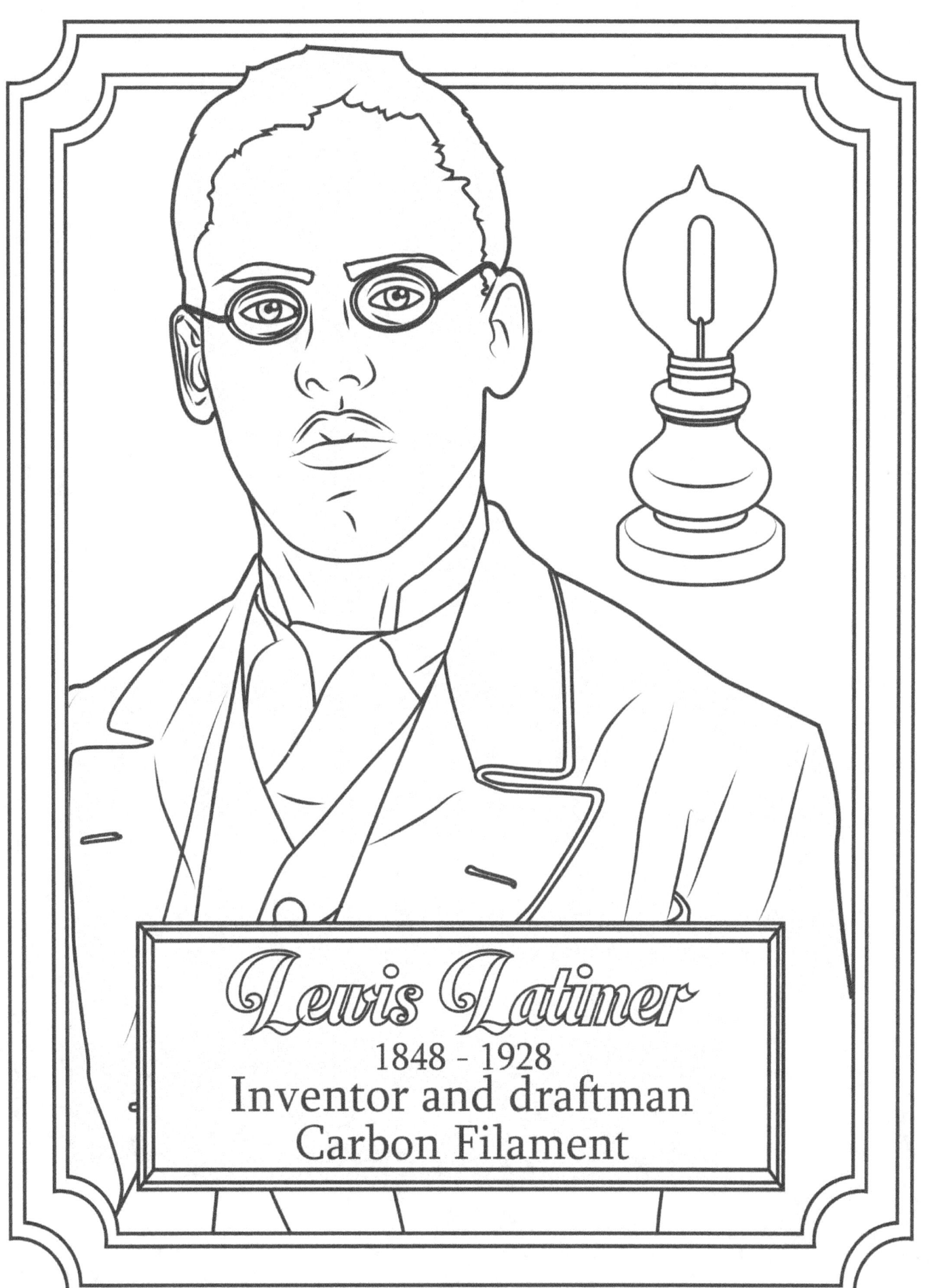

Lewis Latimer
1848 - 1928
Inventor and draftman
Carbon Filament

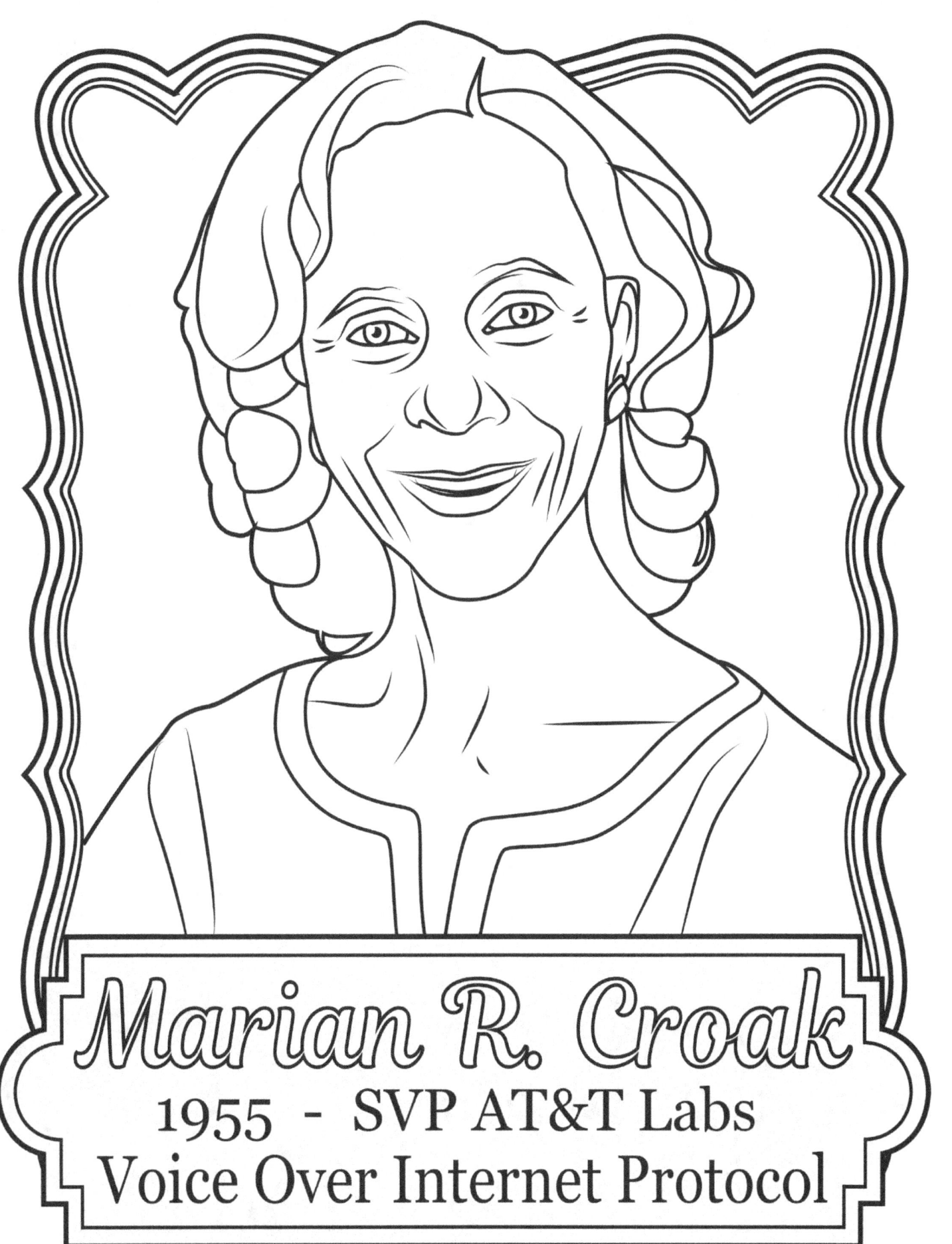

Marian R. Croak

1955 - SVP AT&T Labs
Voice Over Internet Protocol

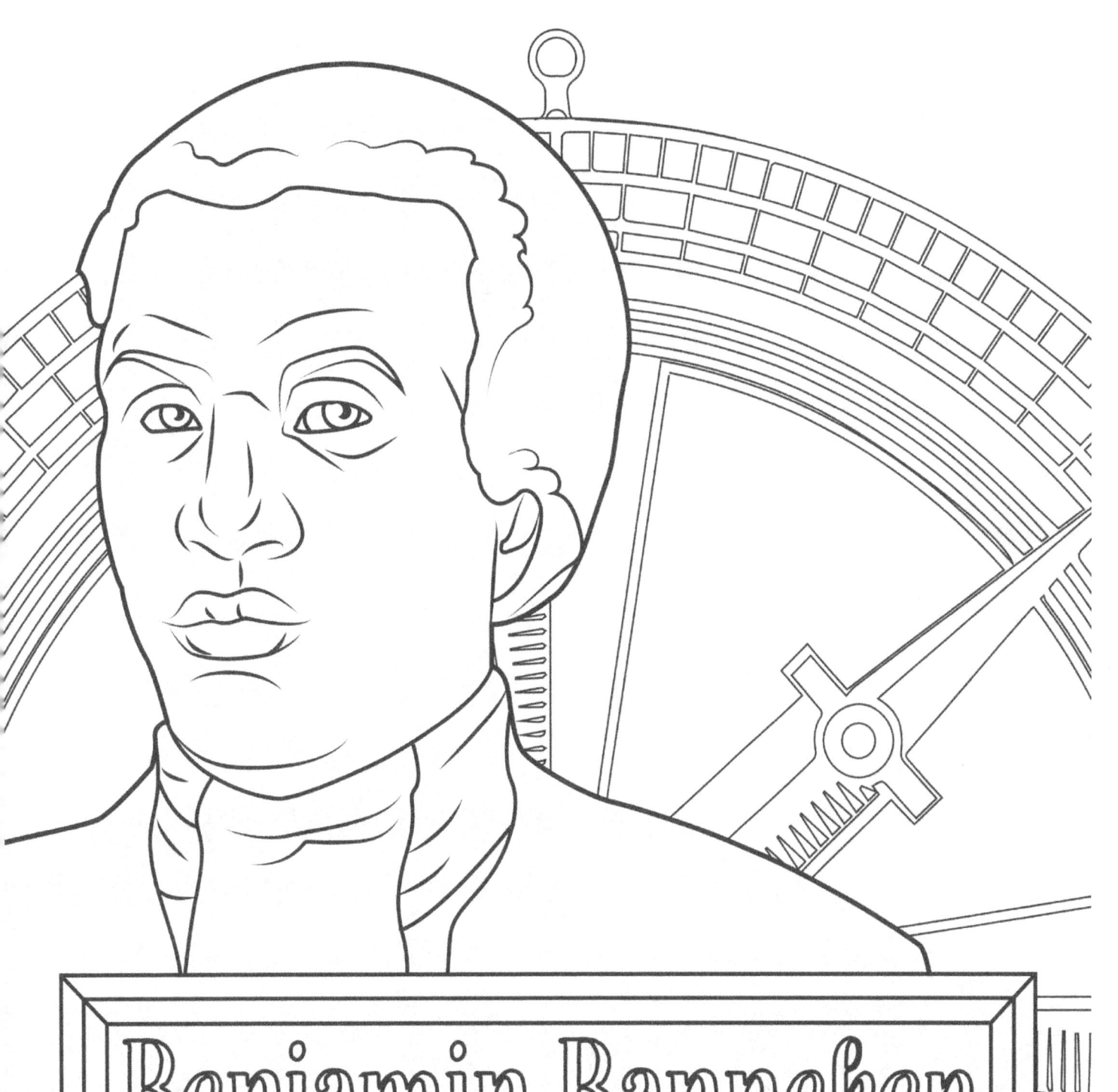

Benjamin Banneker

Astronomer - Inventor

Almanac Author   1731 - 1806

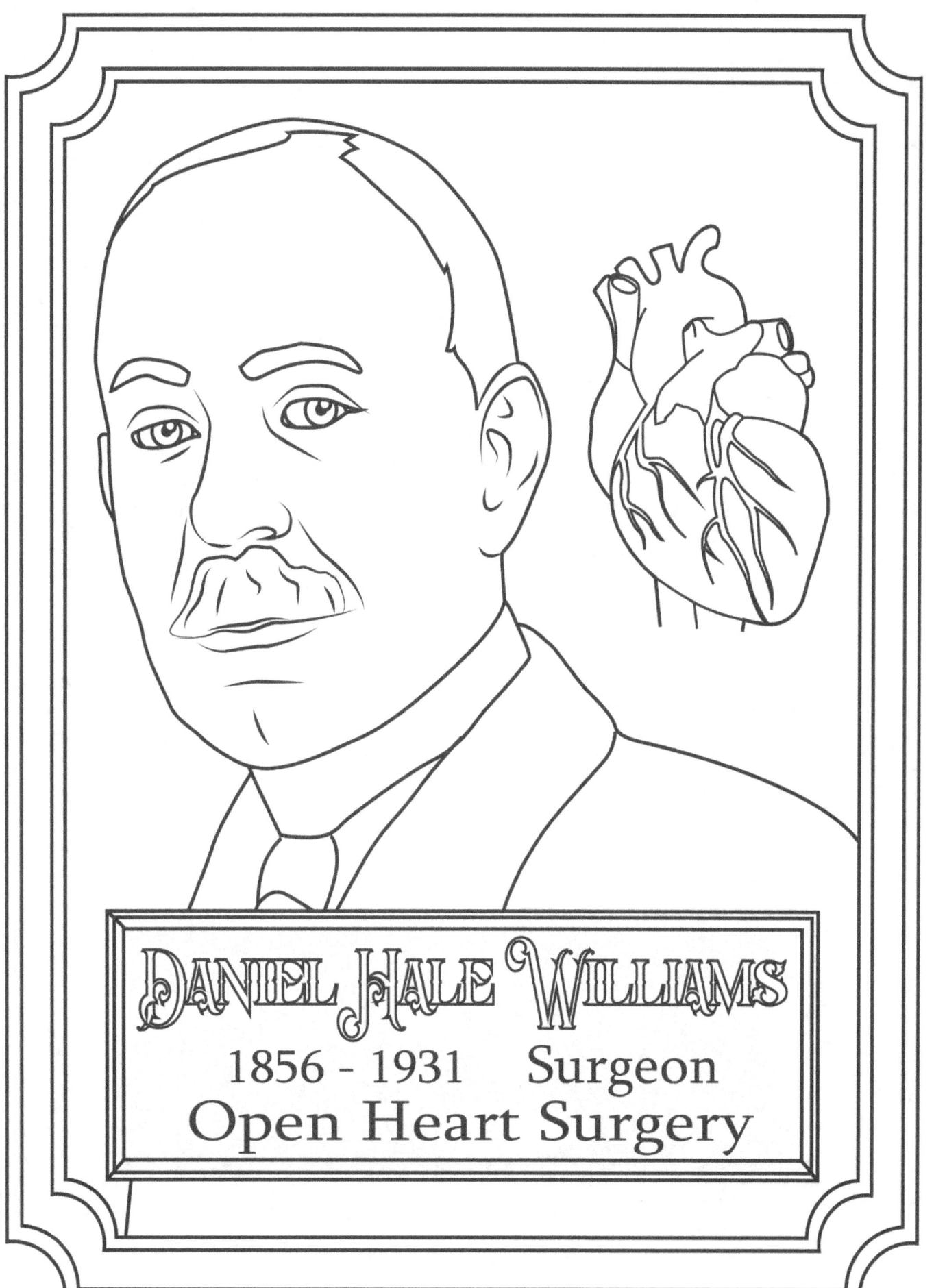

DANIEL HALE WILLIAMS

1856 - 1931   Surgeon
Open Heart Surgery

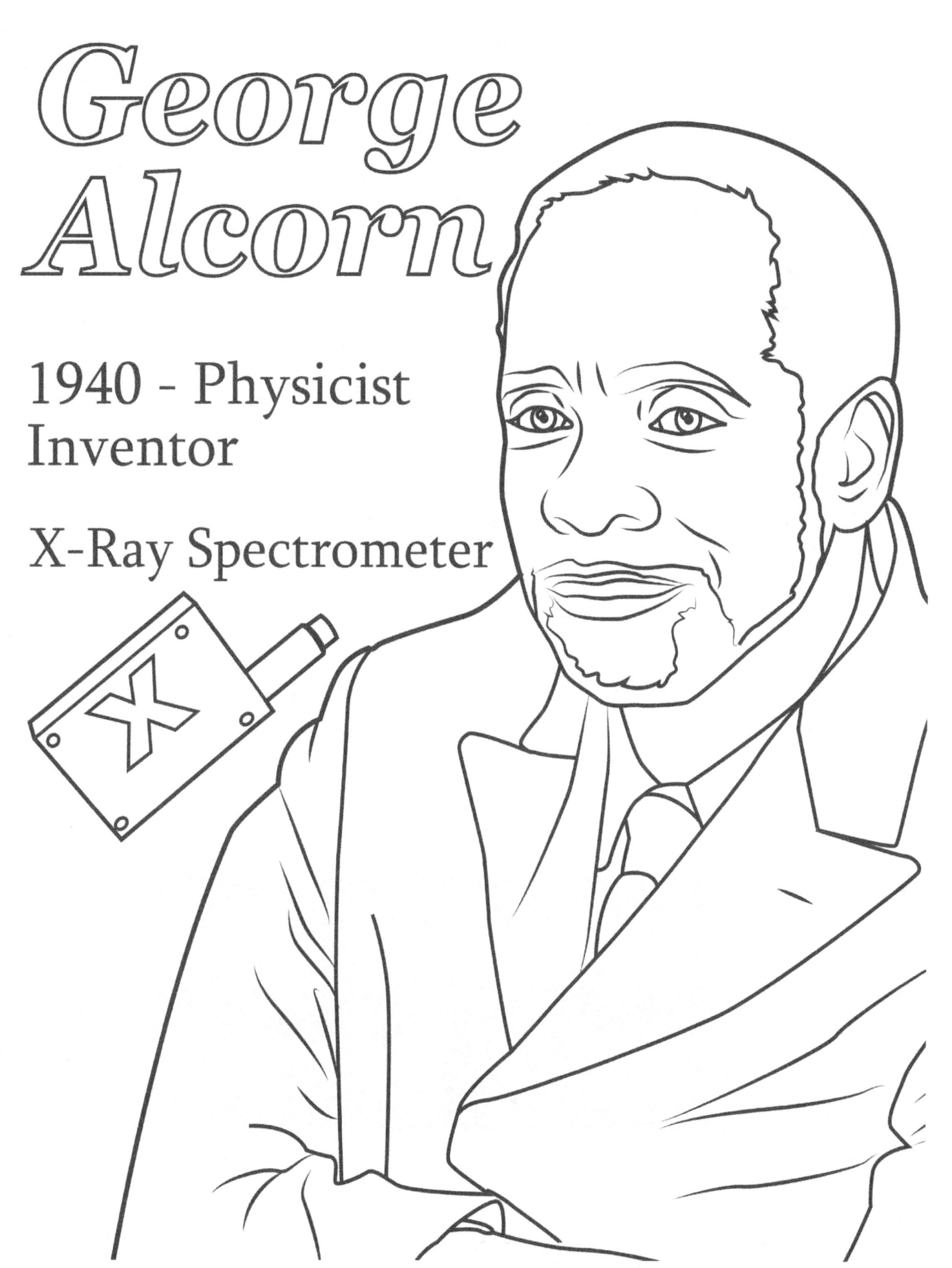

George Alcorn

1940 - Physicist
Inventor

X-Ray Spectrometer

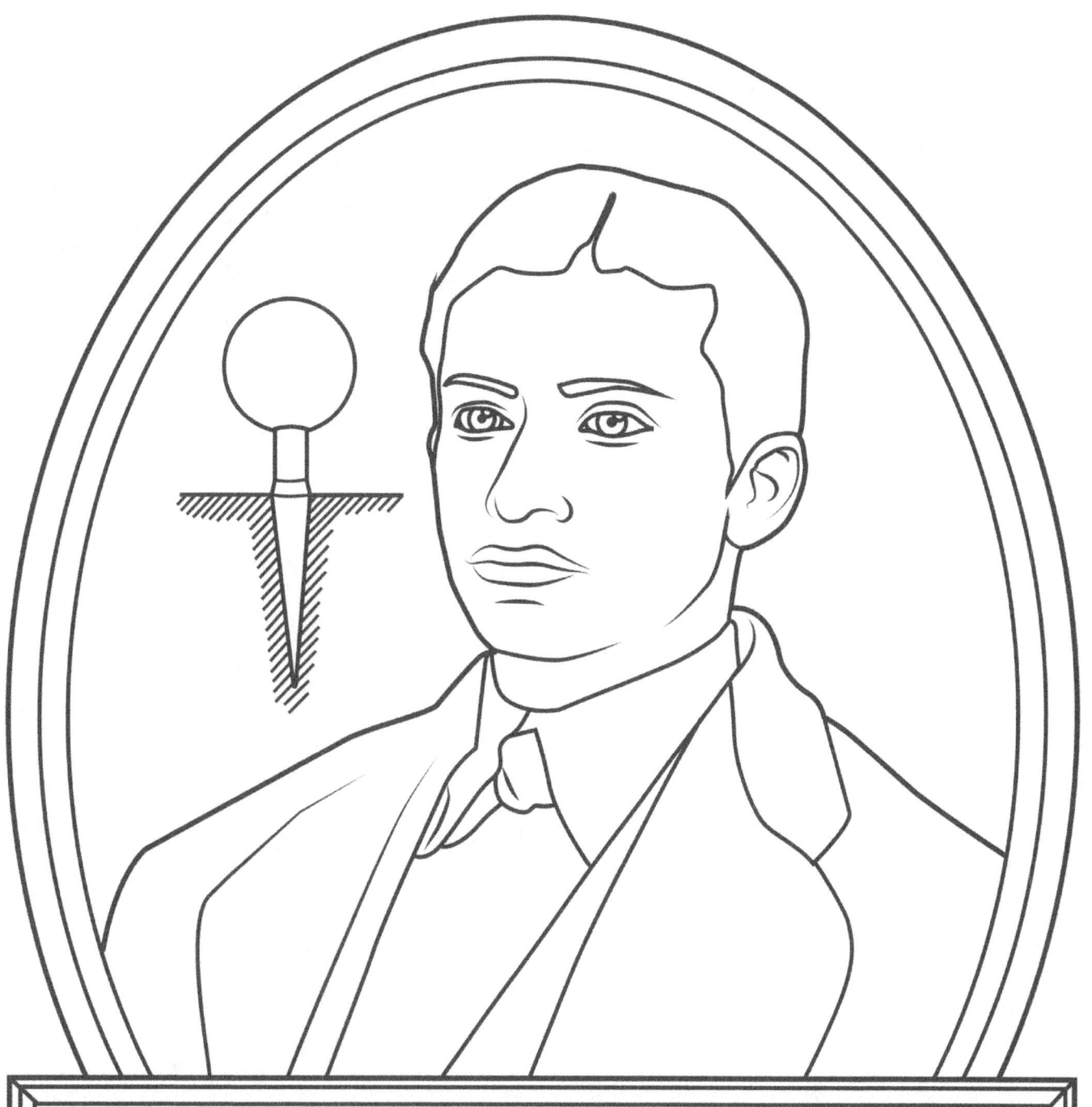

George F. Grant

1846-1910 Academic Dentist Inventor

Improved golf tee

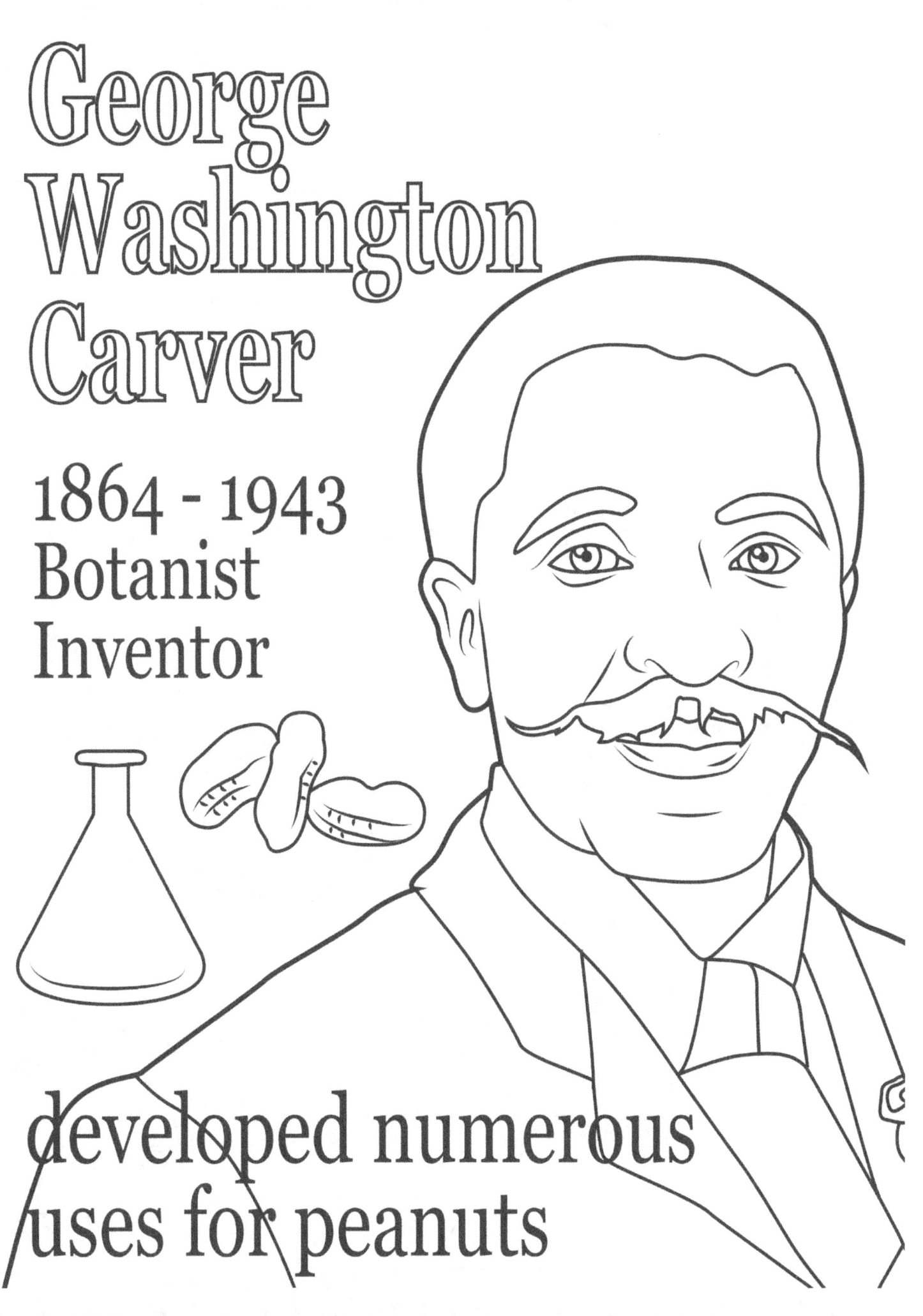

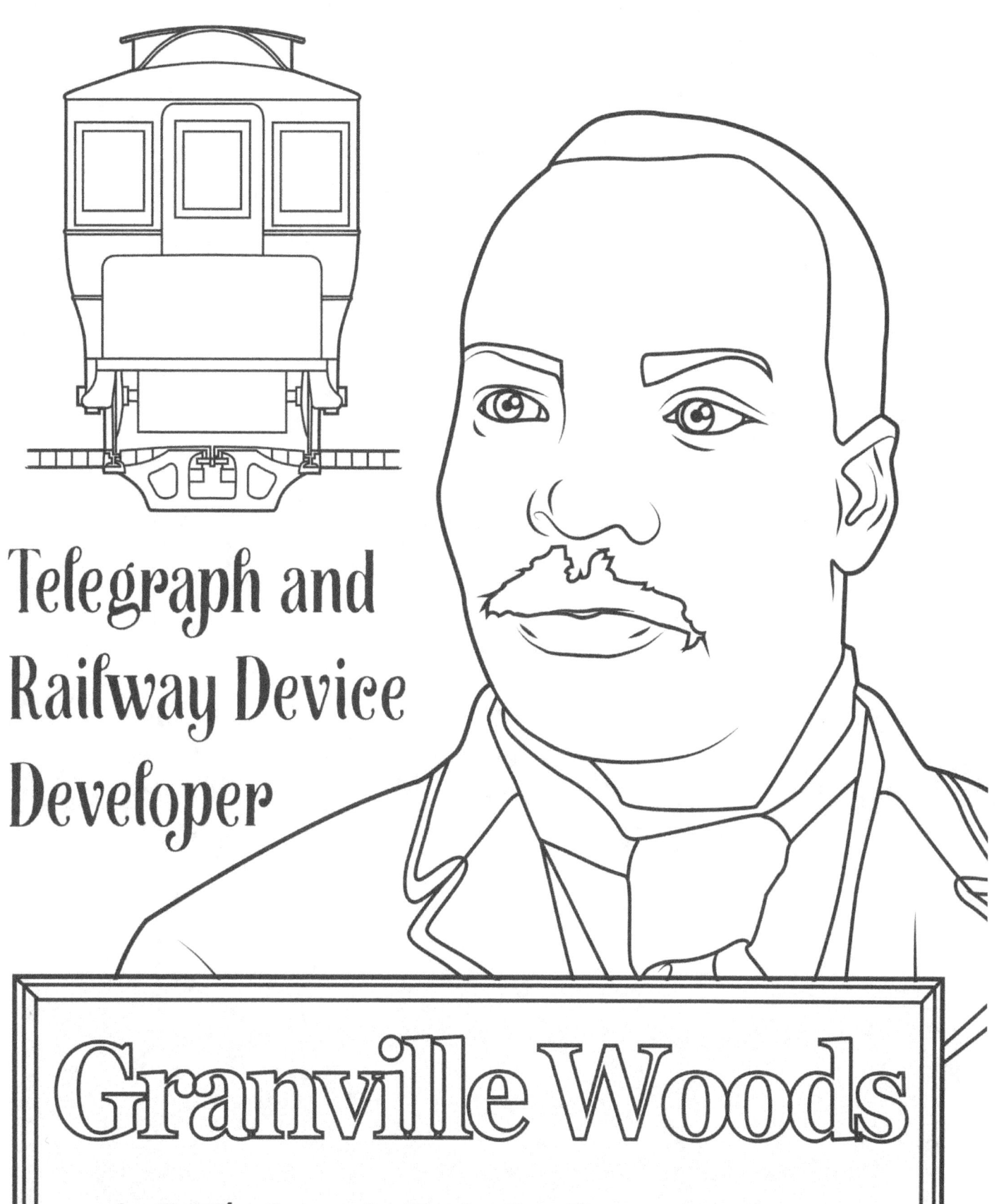

Telegraph and Railway Device Developer

Granville Woods

1856 - 1910 Inventor

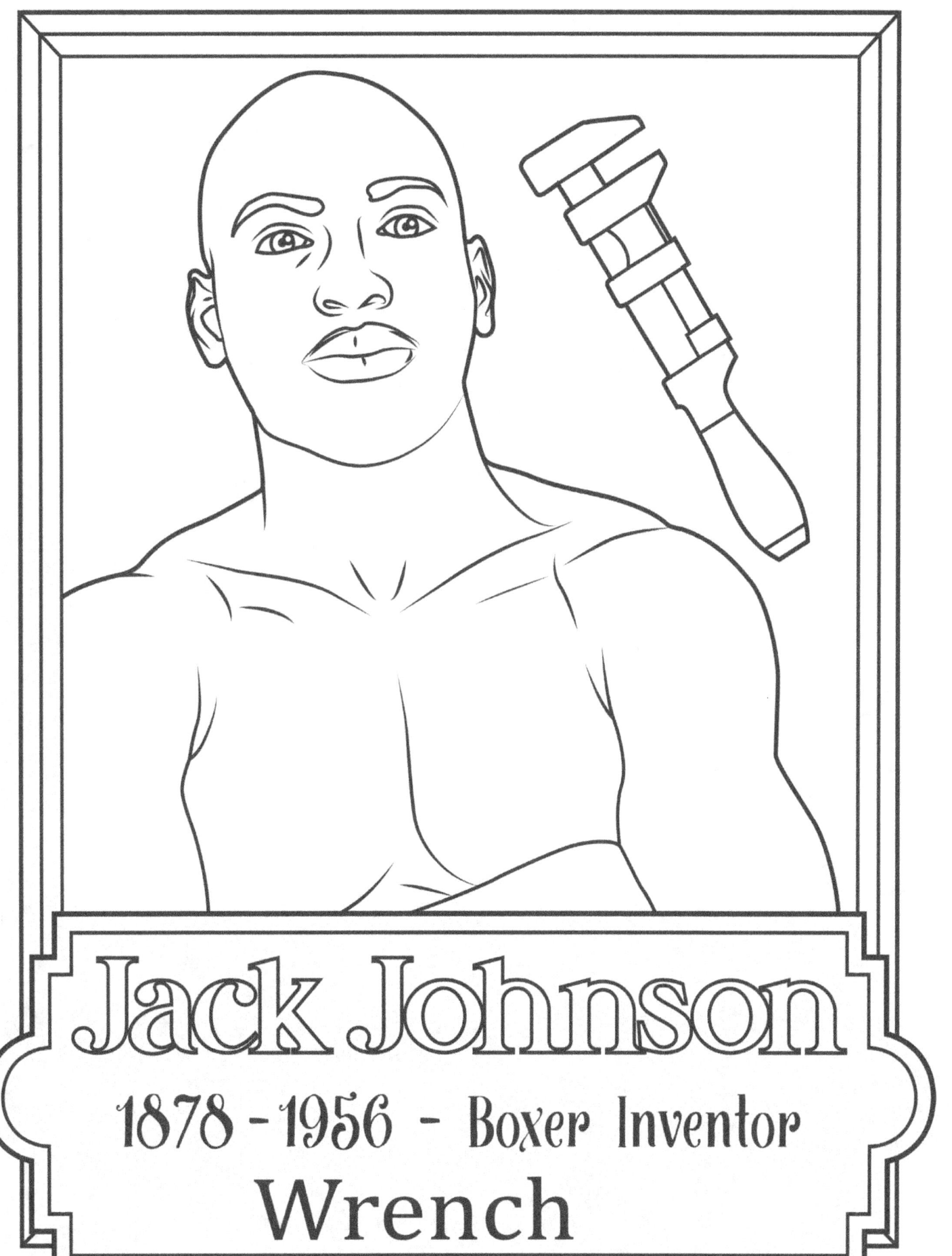

Jack Johnson

1878 - 1956 - Boxer Inventor

Wrench

Madam C. J. Walker

1867 - 1919
Business woman

Hair Products Empire

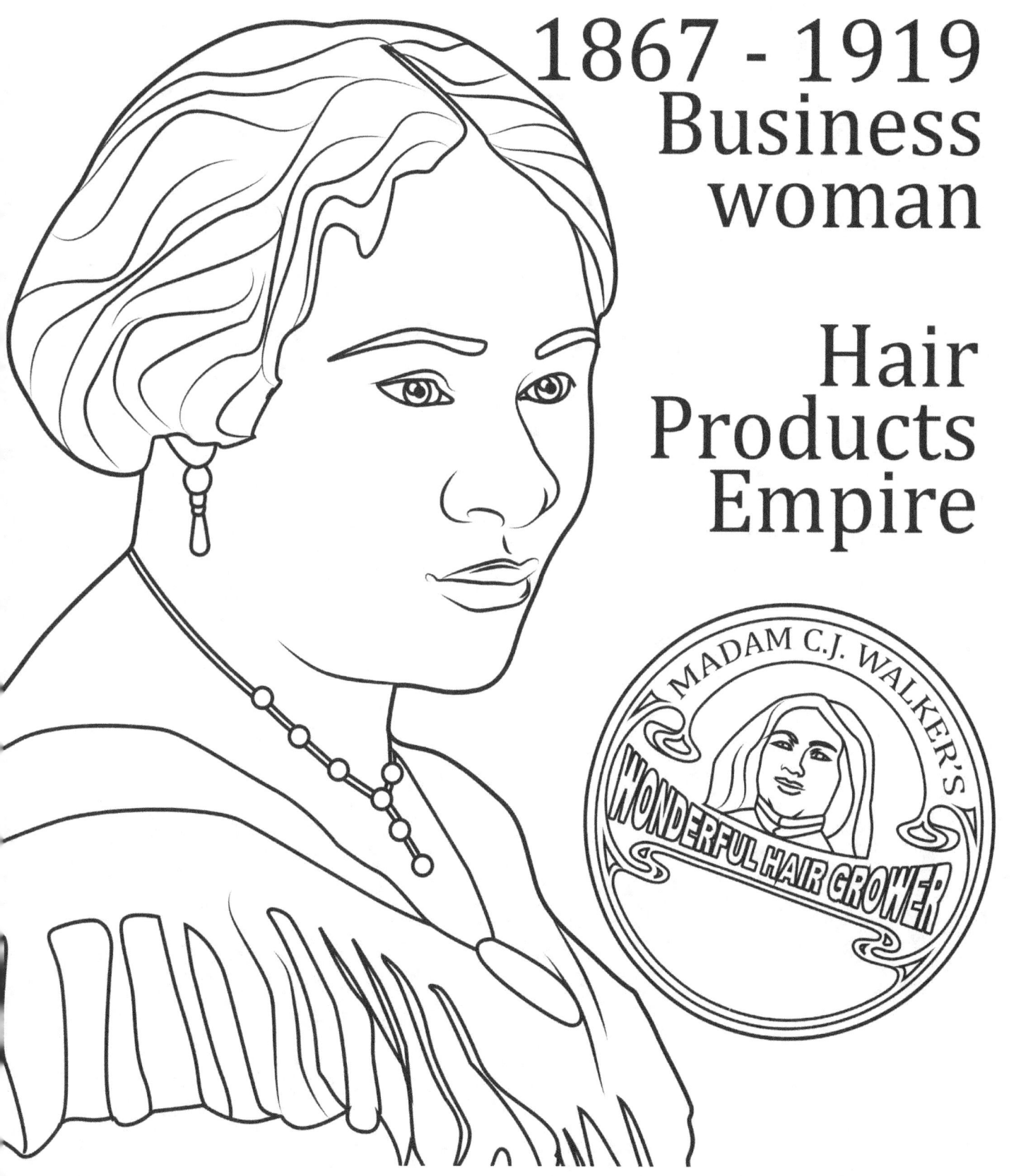

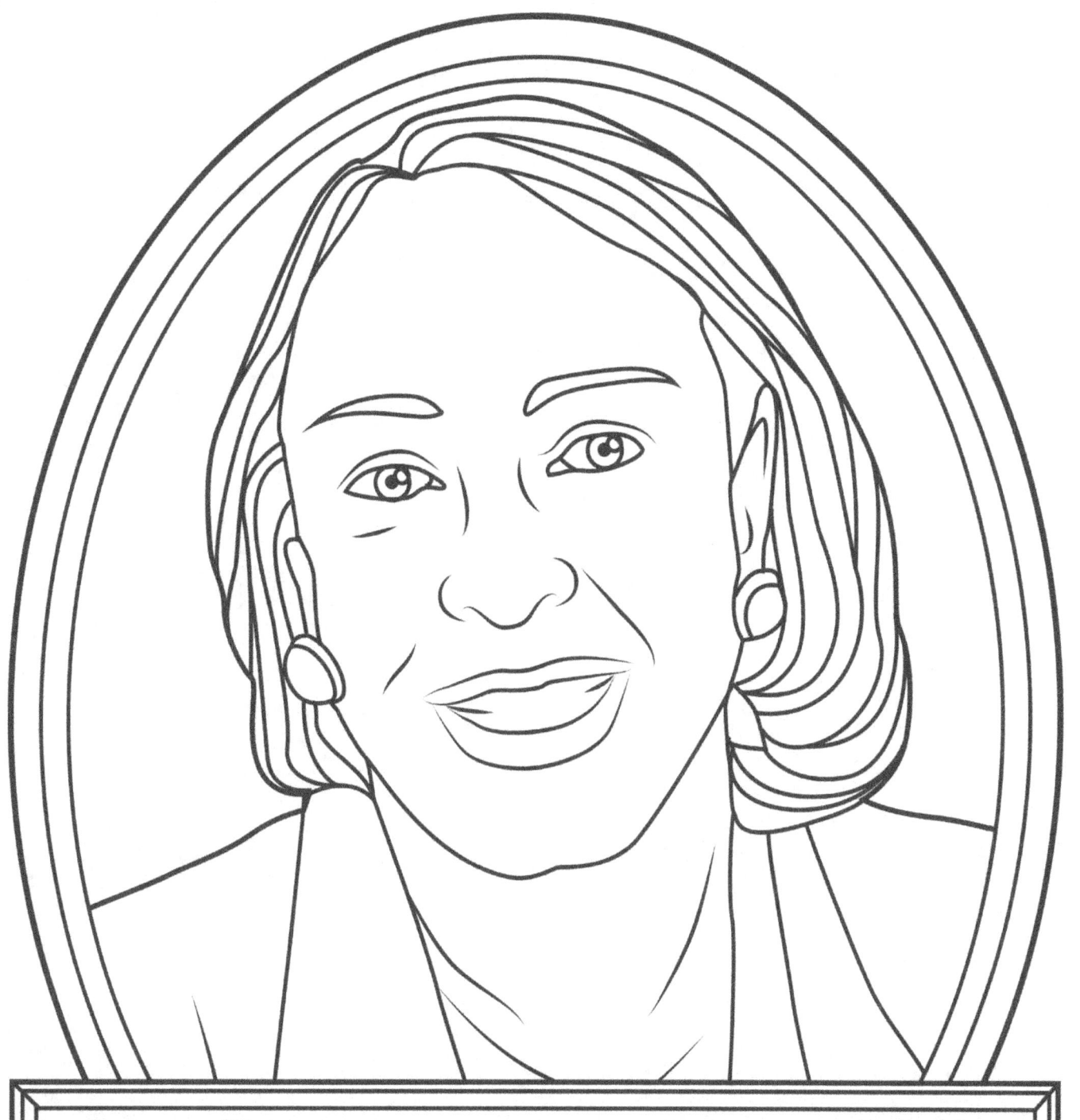

Patricia Bath

1942 - Ophthalmologist, Inventor

Laser Surgical Device

Percy Julian

1899 - 1975 - Chemist

chemical synthesis of medicinal drugs

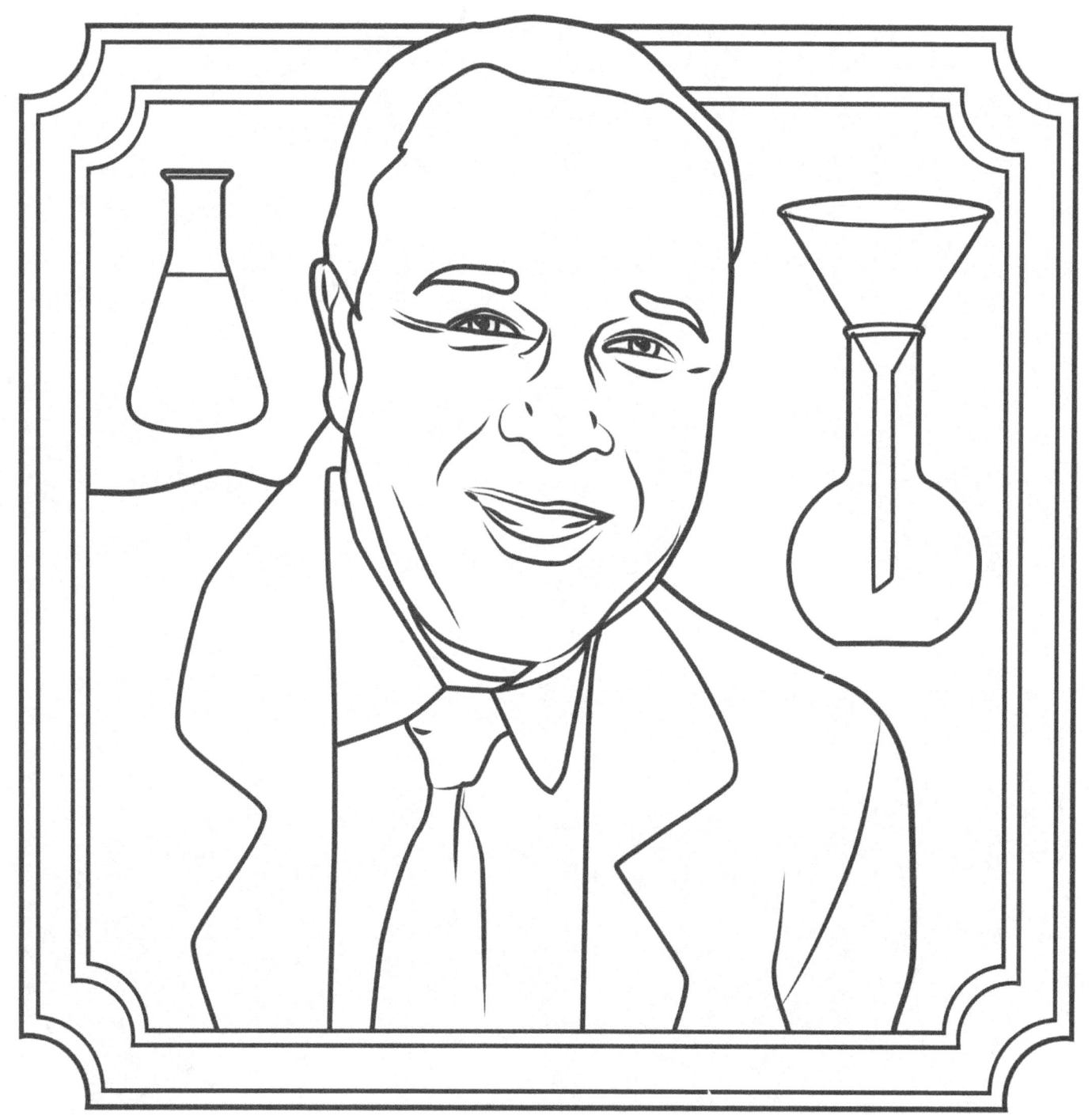

George Carruthers

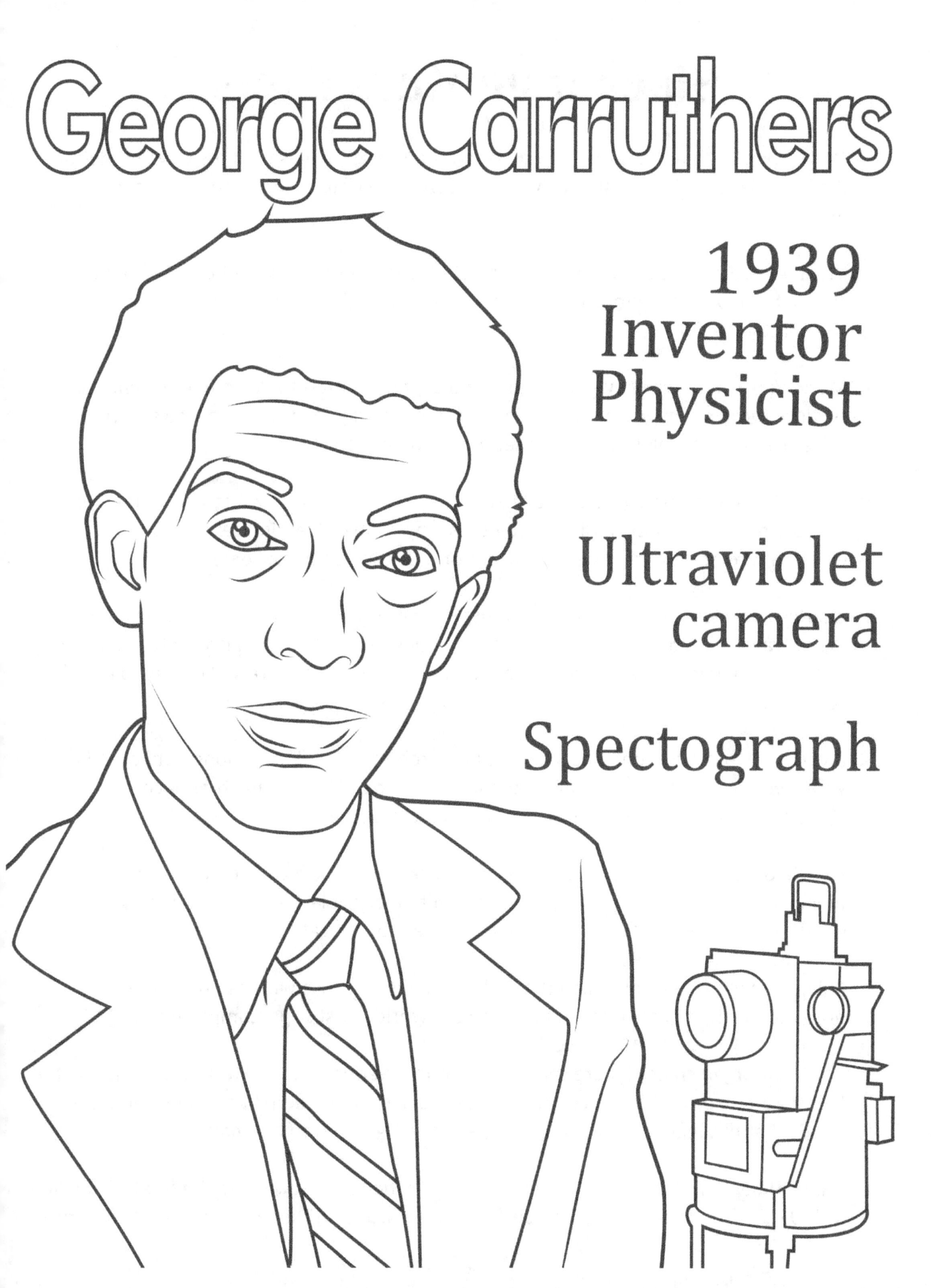

1939
Inventor
Physicist

Ultraviolet
camera

Spectograph

Black Inventors Facts

1. Otis Boykin was an inventor who has saved thousands of lives with the development of the pacemaker. He was also involved in the creation of IBM computers, and chemical air filters.

2. Dr. Shirley Jackson is a theoretical physicist who invented a range of devices that are crucial to modern day life. These include fibre-optic cables, touch tone telephones, caller ID, and call waiting.

3. Marie Van Brittan Brown was a full-time nurse, but wanted to do something about security threats around her home. This led to her designing the first home security system and the development of closed-circuit television.

4. Lonnie G. Johnson was an aerospace engineer for NASA, and although he worked on a number of important exploration projects such as the Galileo Jupiter Probe and the Mars Observer Project, his most famous invention was the Super Soaker water gun.

5. Charles Drew was an American doctor during the second world war, and developed blood transfusion techniques that saved countless lives. His work also led to the creation of the first blood bank and blood transportation vehicles that are still crucial to health services to this day.

6. If you've ever made a phone call across the internet instead of a phone network, then you have Marian Croak to thank. She holds more than 200 patents that have made significant improvements in communication technologies.

7. Lisa Gelobter created a technology called Shockwave, which allowed people to make online animations. Without this, GIFs wouldn't be possible, and she now works as the Chief Digital Service Officer in the US department of education.

8. Philip Emeagwali is often called the 'Bill Gates of Africa'. He was inspired by the honeycombs that bees produce to create the world's first supercomputer in 1989.

9. Garrett Morgan created more than 50 different inventions in his lifetime, but his most famous are ones that saved countless lives. He designed the first gas mask, the safety hoods that firefighters wear, and also the amber light in traffic signals.

10. Daniel Hale Williams was an American surgeon who founded the first integrated hospital in 1891, and in the following year performed the world's first ever open heart surgery.

11. George Washington Carver worked for the agricultural department in Alabama, and conducted studies to determine which crop was the best for local farmers to grow. He created more than 300 products from peanuts, including laundry soaps and fuels, which led to it becoming the second most valuable crop in the southern states of America by 1940.

12. In the late 1800s if you wanted to use an elevator you would have to manually open two sets of doors before getting in or out. This posed a real safety risk until automatic doors were invented by Alexander Miles in 1887. The principles of his design are still the ones used today!

13. Dr. James E West worked for Bell Laboratories, and during this time he developed the Electroacoustic Transducer Electret Microphone. This technology is now used in ninety percent of the microphones that are used today.

14. The first African American person to receive a patent in the United States was Thomas L. Jennings. He registered his designs for a form of dry cleaning in 1821.

15. Madam C.J Walker is often called 'America's first female self made millionaire'. She designed haircare products, and oversaw a business empire that included beauty schools, salons, and training schools across the U.S.

16. George Carruthers was an astrophysicist who worked for the U.S. government and NASA. He designed an important piece of technology called an ultraviolet spectrograph, and this enabled astronaut to conduct important experiments in space.

17. Dr. Patricia Bath patented a medical procedure in 1988 that improved the success of eye operations. Thanks to her, the eyesight of millions of people has been made better.

18. We take them for granted now, but in the 19th century, most people in America weren't able to afford shoes. Jan Ernst Matzeliger invented a machine that would change all that. It attached the sole of the shoe to the upper part, and was able to produce 700 pairs of shoes per day, while the pervious method could only make 50.

19. Lewis Latimer was born in 1848, and worked with Thomas Edison and Alexander Graham Bell. It was because of his invention of the carbon filament that light bulbs were possible, and he also played a crucial role in the development of the telephone.

20. The best inventions improve the quality of people's lives, and that's exactly what Mary and Mildred Davidson wanted to do. They created walker frames to allow people with mobility difficulties to move around, and they also designed the toilet paper holder.

Black History Month Word Search

Can you find all of the hidden words?

```
S P E C T O G R A P H J F I B
V Q T B H V Z F A Z E P L X O
Q Z A U G E F H P I S Q M Z Z
P Q N D I A R E V R L L M D Q
S B X T L Y E R Y Y O L Z Z D
K Y Q K C T E I G C K T K U B
R T Q C I V D T L I G E E U V
A I U J F A O A N W E L A S V
P L O Z F Q M G N Z P O Z U T
A A C H A R L E S D R E W E L
S U P E R S O A K E R N N V J
O Q Q N T M N U Q H R M S S L
R E K A M E C A P X F L U W M
K L L B Z K V F W L S T U K J
I X F A G Y N Z S Y W Y L Q W
```

Charles Drew   Heritage   Pacemaker   Spectograph
Equality   M L King   Protest   Super Soaker
Freedom   Malcolm X   Rosa Parks   Traffic Light

Black History Inventors Quiz

Questions

1. What type of water pistol did Lonnie G. Johnson create?
2. In what year was the first supercomputer built?
3. Thomas L. Jennings was the first African American to receive what in 1821?
4. How many shoes could Jan Ernst Matzeliger's machine make in one day?
5. Automatic doors were developed in 1887 to be used where?
6. What was the profession of the woman who created home security systems?
7. Charles Drew invented methods for blood transfusion during which war?
8. What is the nickname of Philip Emeagwali?
9. In which year was the world's first open heart surgery performed?
10. Before Garrett Morgan's invention, how many colours were there on traffic lights?
11. George Washington Carver created products from Peanuts while working for the government in which US state?
12. Dr Shirley Jackson was the first African American woman to earn a doctorate in nuclear physics from which famous American University in Cambridge, Massachusetts?
13. What was the life-saving invention that was designed by Otis Boykin?
14. Elijah McCoy developed techniques that would revolutionise which method of transport?
15. G.E Becket received a patent in 1892 for which object that's essential for sending post?
16. What did Sarah Boone design in 1892 that is used to help remove wrinkles from clothes? Before this invention, people often used a plank of wood between two chairs.
17. In 1900, J.F. Pickering created a design for which type of flying vehicle that's rarely used anymore?
18. In which century did J. Ricks patent the horseshoe?
19. In 1896, J.T. White invented which device used to remove the juice from a yellow citrus fruit?
20. Lloyd Hall, who developed a series of food preservation techniques, had a degree in what?

Black History Month Crossword

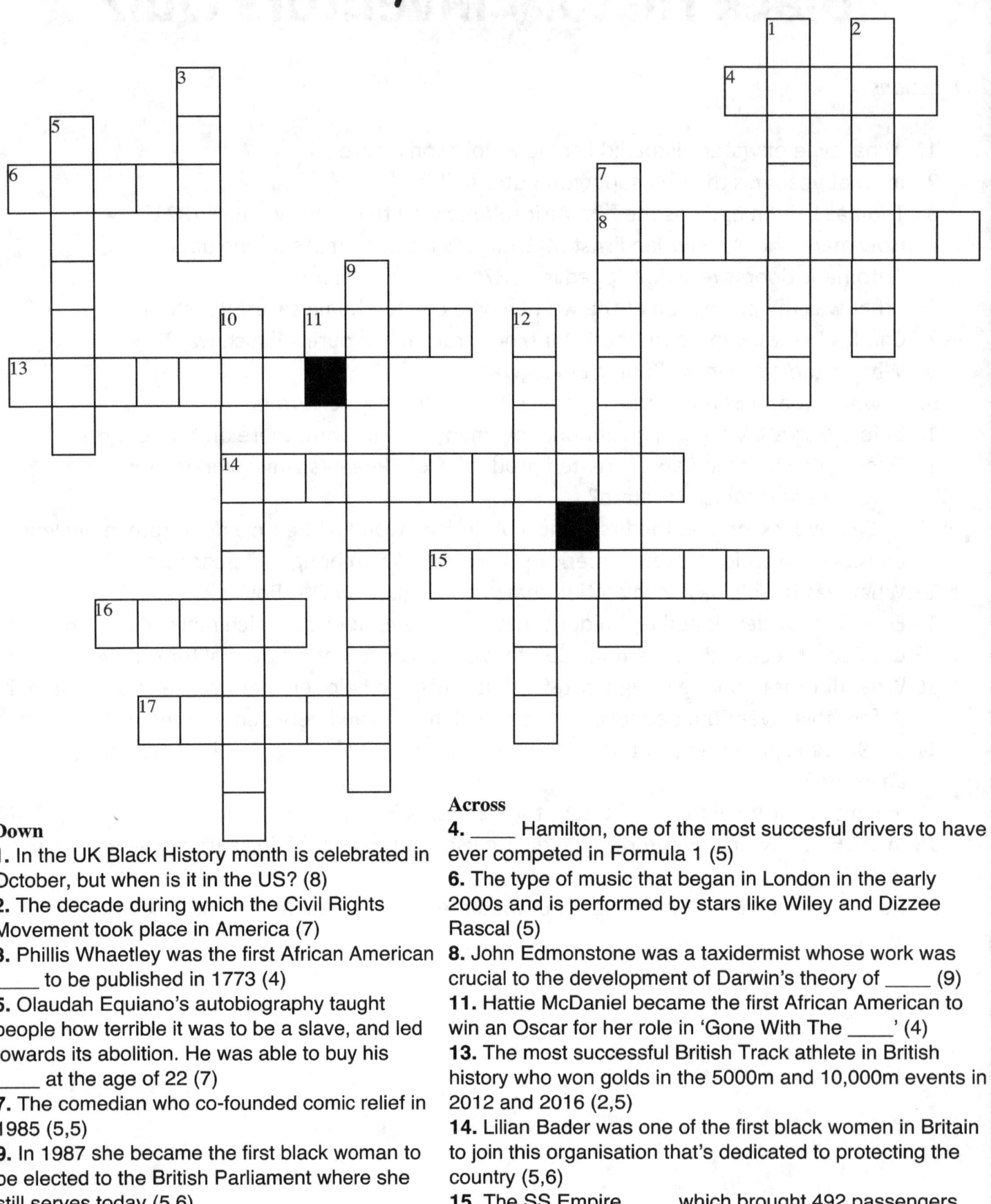

Down

1. In the UK Black History month is celebrated in October, but when is it in the US? (8)

2. The decade during which the Civil Rights Movement took place in America (7)

3. Phillis Whaetley was the first African American _____ to be published in 1773 (4)

5. Olaudah Equiano's autobiography taught people how terrible it was to be a slave, and led towards its abolition. He was able to buy his _____ at the age of 22 (7)

7. The comedian who co-founded comic relief in 1985 (5,5)

9. In 1987 she became the first black woman to be elected to the British Parliament where she still serves today (5,6)

10. The first African American to become US President (6,5)

12. Guion Stewart Bluford Jr. was the first African American to become an _____ for NASA (9)

Across

4. _____ Hamilton, one of the most succesful drivers to have ever competed in Formula 1 (5)

6. The type of music that began in London in the early 2000s and is performed by stars like Wiley and Dizzee Rascal (5)

8. John Edmonstone was a taxidermist whose work was crucial to the development of Darwin's theory of _____ (9)

11. Hattie McDaniel became the first African American to win an Oscar for her role in 'Gone With The _____' (4)

13. The most successful British Track athlete in British history who won golds in the 5000m and 10,000m events in 2012 and 2016 (2,5)

14. Lilian Bader was one of the first black women in Britain to join this organisation that's dedicated to protecting the country (5,6)

15. The SS Empire _____ which brought 492 passengers from the Caribbean to the UK in 1948 (8)

16. Charles Drew invented a bank for this vital resource (5)

17. George Washington Carver found different ways to use this seed that's also known as a monkey nut (6)

Spot The Difference

6 Differences to Spot. Can You Spot Them All?

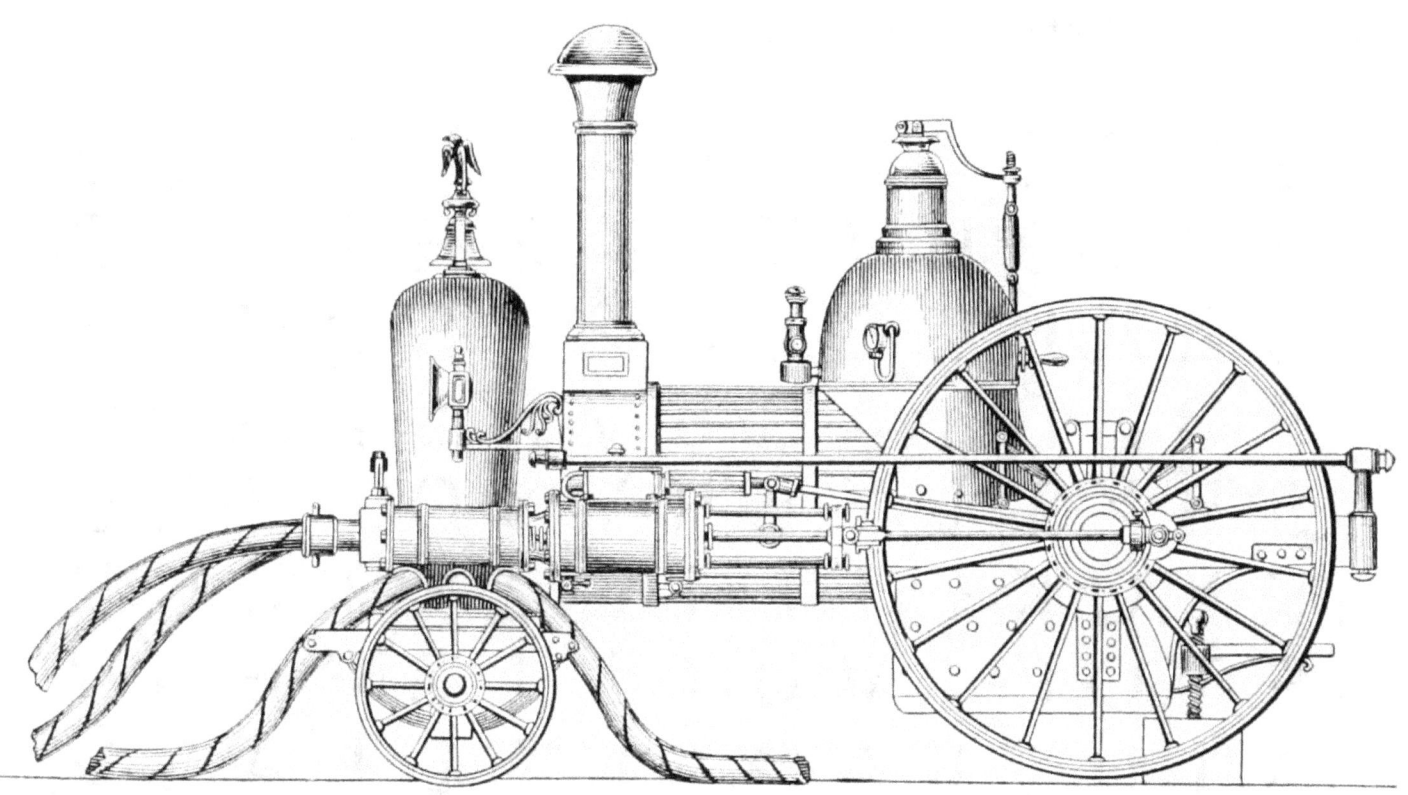

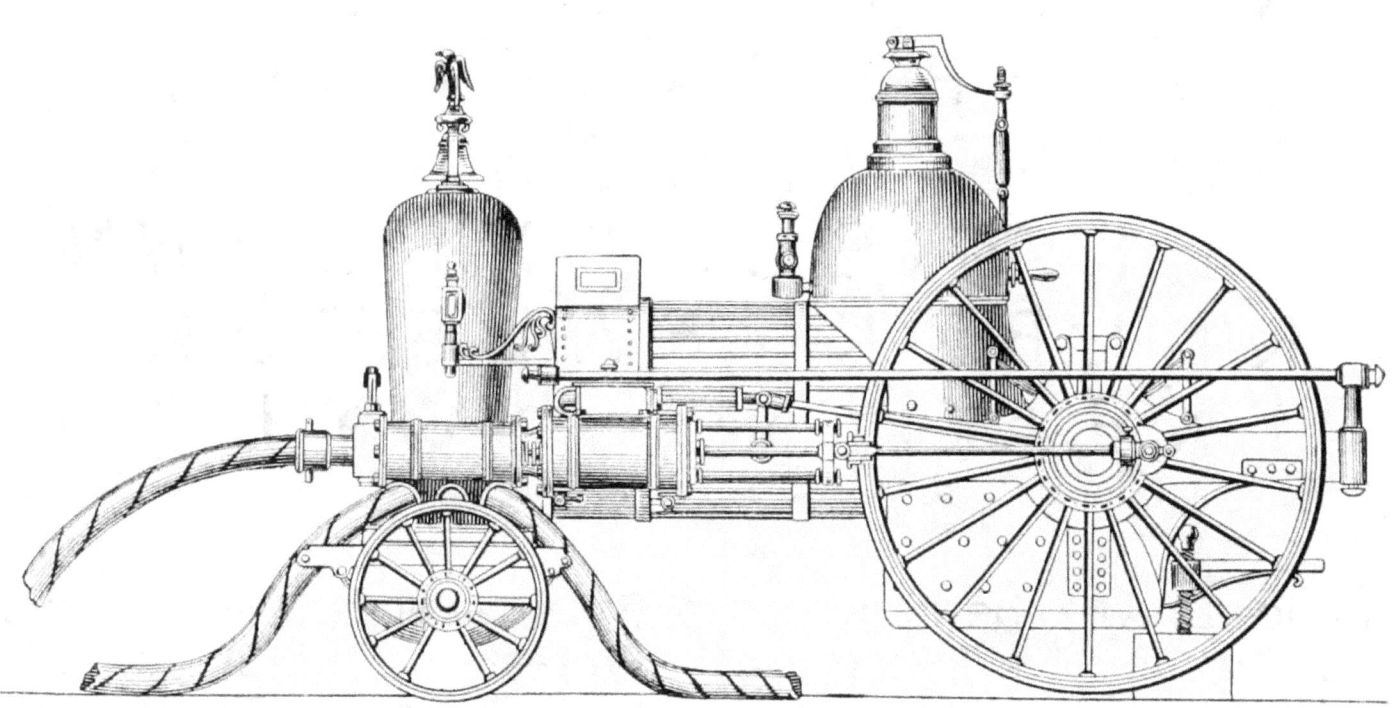

Black History Month Word Search

Can you find all of the hidden words?

```
S P E C T O G R A P H J F I B
V Q T B H V Z F A Z E P L X O
Q Z A U G E F H P I S Q M Z Z
P Q N D I A R E V R L L M D Q
S B X T L Y E R Y Y O L Z Z D
K Y Q K C T E I G C K T K U B
R T Q C I V D T L I G E E U V
A I U J F A O A N W E L A S V
P L O Z F Q M G N Z P O Z U T
A A C H A R L E S D R E W E L
S U P E R S O A K E R N N V J
O Q Q N T M N U Q H R M S S L
R E K A M E C A P X F L U W M
K L L B Z K V F W L S T U K J
I X F A G Y N Z S Y W Y L Q W
```

Charles Drew	Heritage	Pacemaker	Spectograph
Equality	M L King	Protest	Super Soaker
Freedom	Malcolm X	Rosa Parks	Traffic Light

Answers

1. The Super Soaker
2. 1989
3. A Patent
4. 700
5. Elevator/Lift
6. Nurse
7. World War 2
8. The Bill Gates of Africa
9. 1892
10. 2 (red and green)
11. Alabama
12. MIT (Massachusetts Institute of Technology)
13. Pacemaker
14. Railways
15. Letter Box
16. Ironing Board
17. Airship
18. 19th Century (1885)
19. Lemon Squeezer
20. Chemistry

Spot the Difference

1. One of the front hoses
2. The Chimney
3. Pressure Gauge
4. Front Light
5. Spoke of Front Wheel
6. Bolt to the Right of the Front Wheel

Thank you for purchasing this book.

If you would like to know more about Aryla Publishing Books please visit:-

www.ArylaPublishing.com

Or follow us on
Facebook
Twitter
Instagram
for *free promotions*

@arylapublishing

We would love to know what you think of this book so please leave us a review.

Have a wonderful day ☺

Other Coloring Books from Aryla Publishing

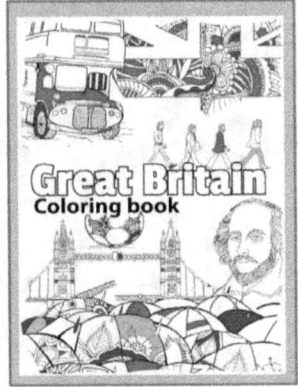
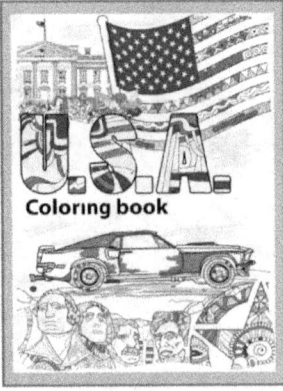
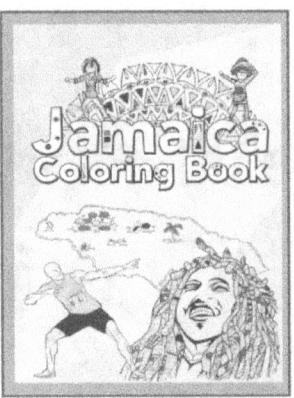
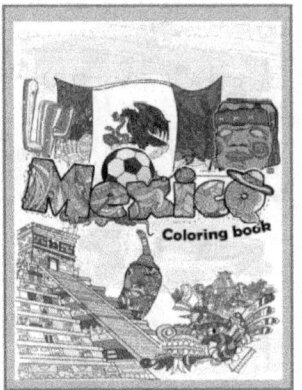

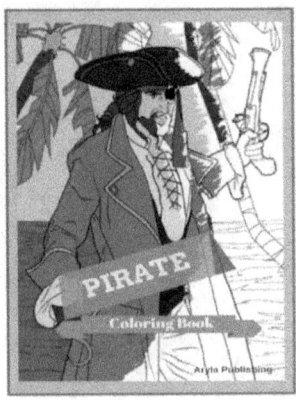
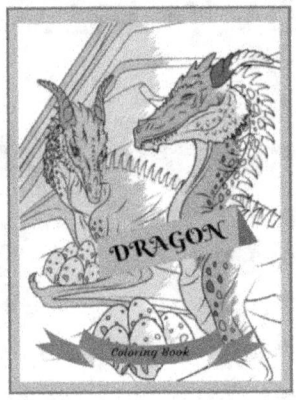
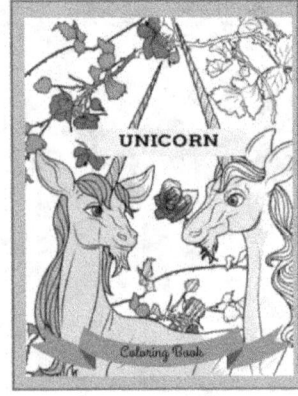
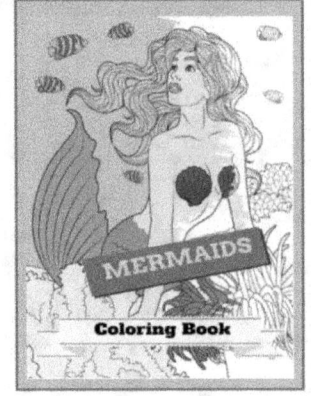

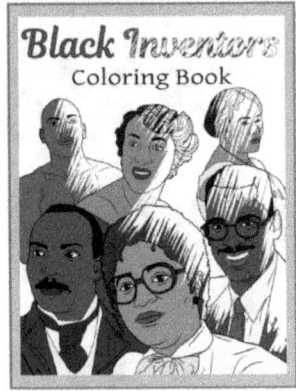
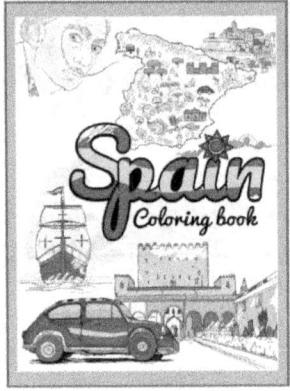
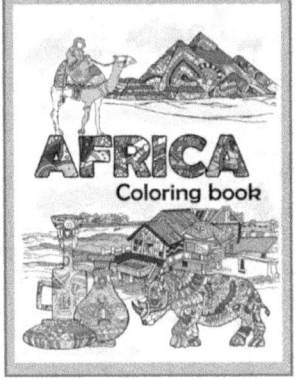
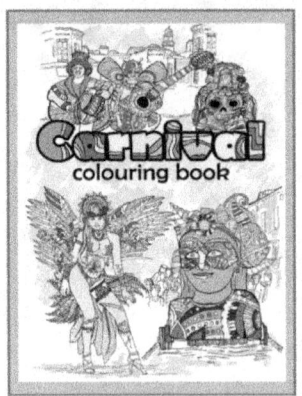

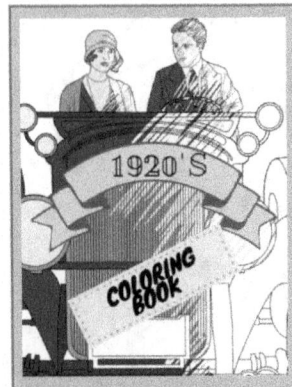
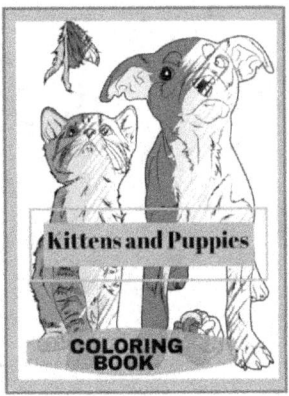
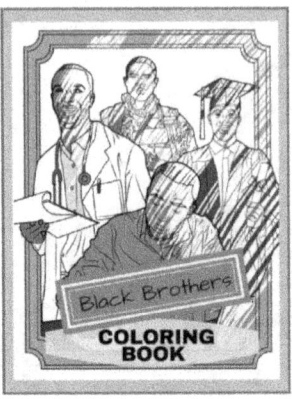
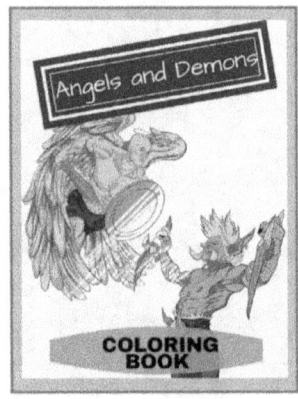

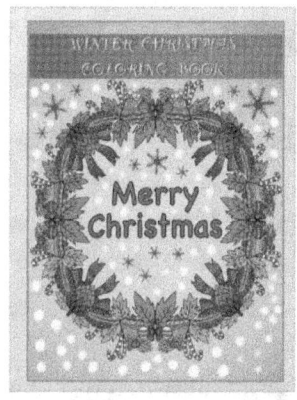
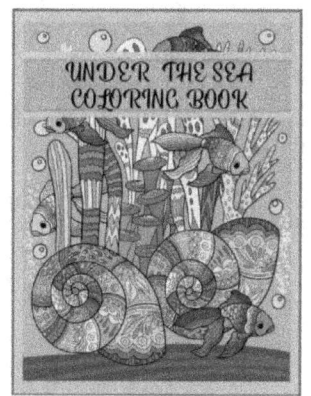
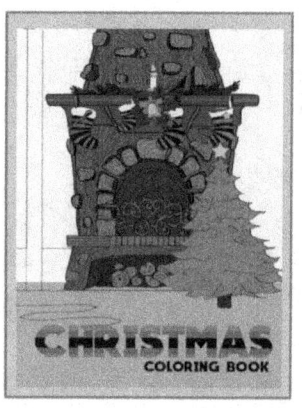
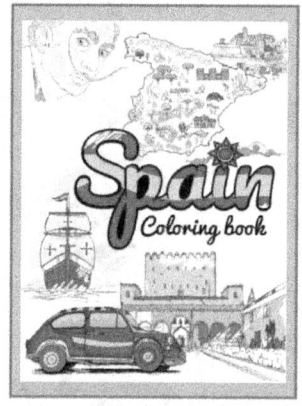
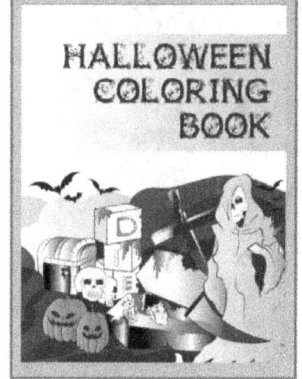
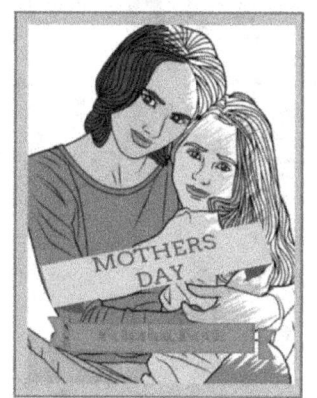
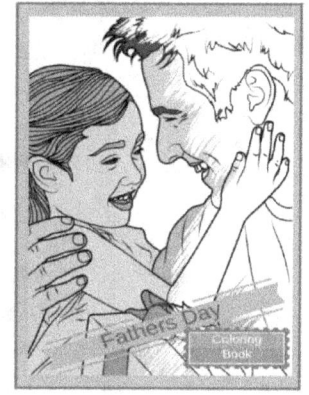
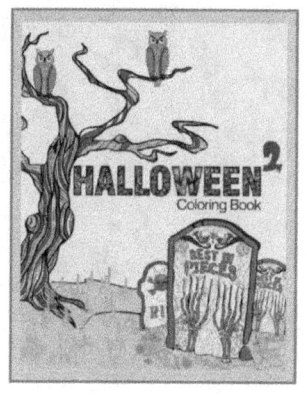
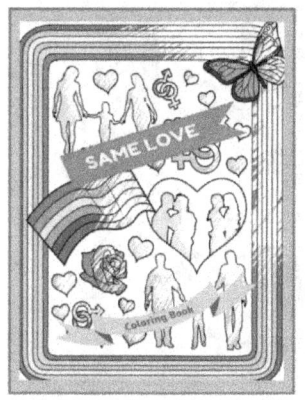
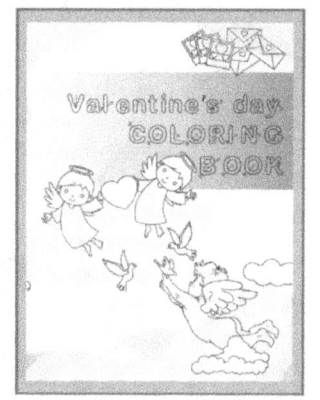
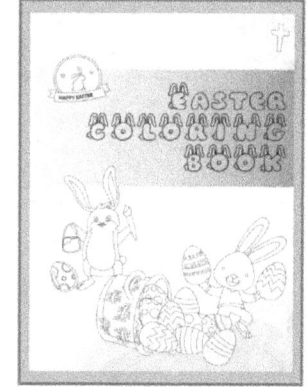
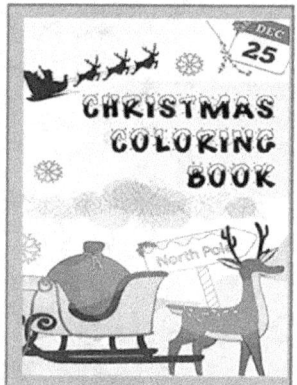

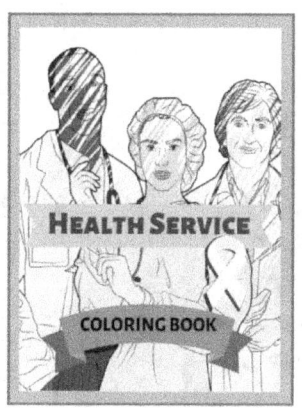
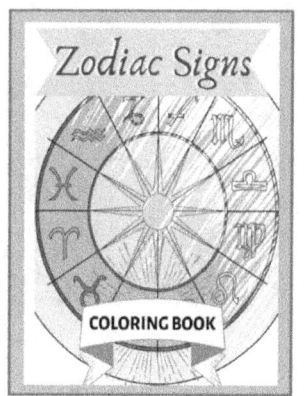
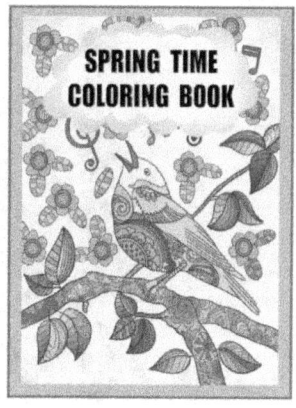

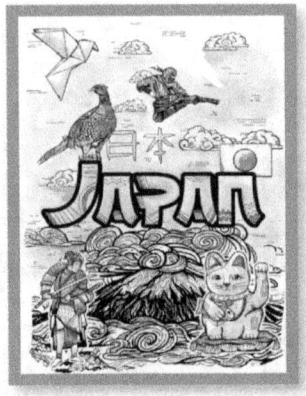
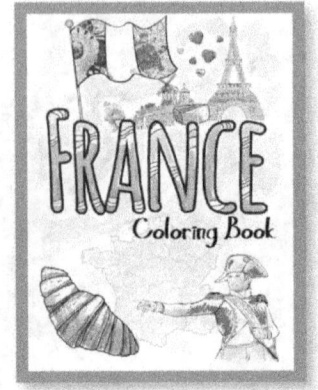
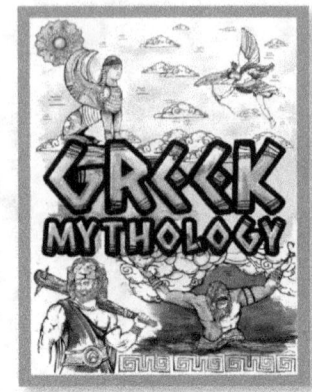
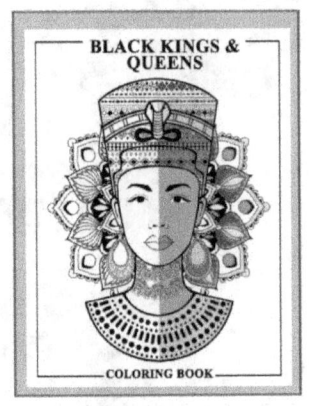
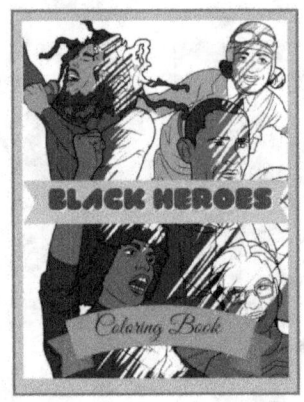
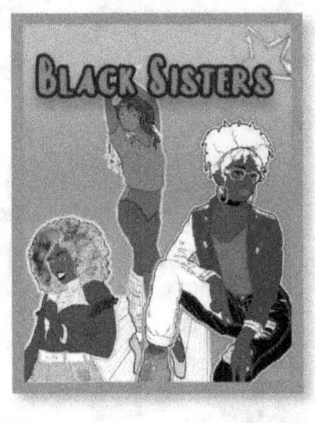
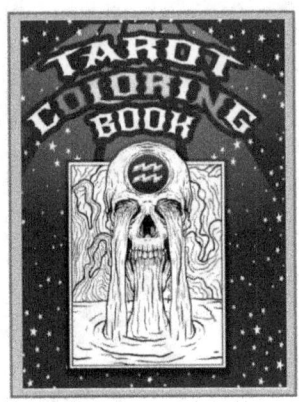
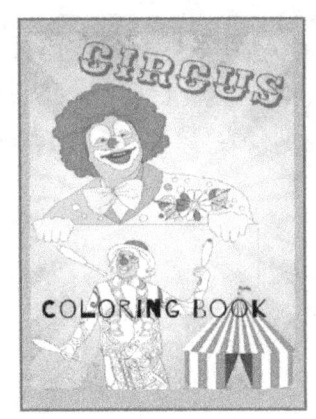
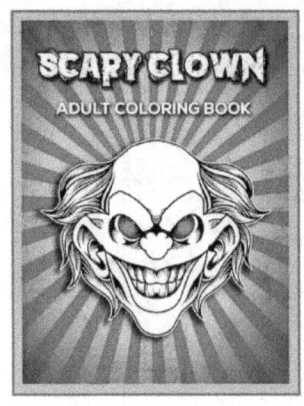
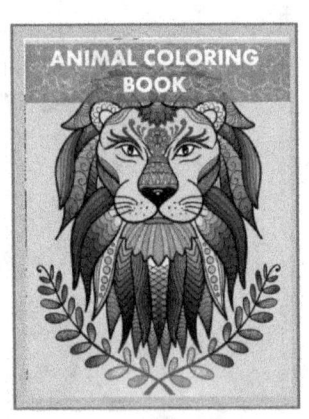
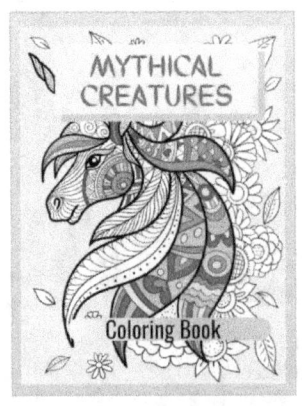
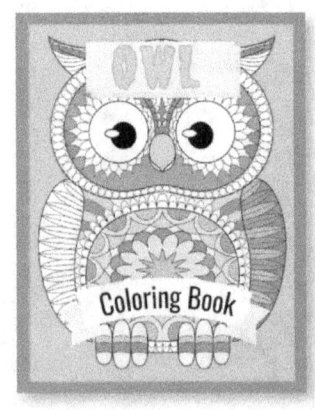

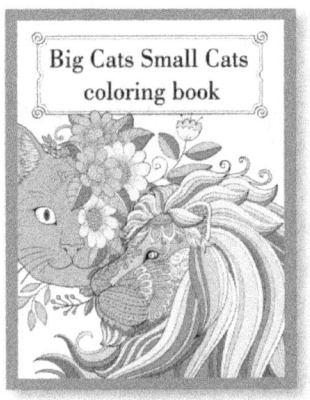

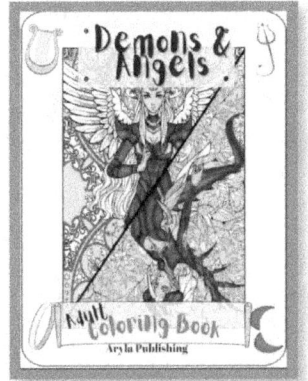

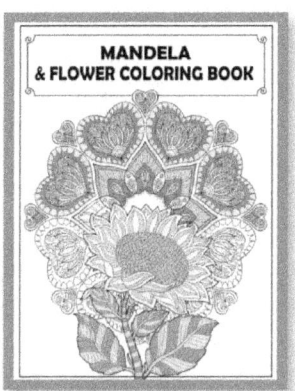

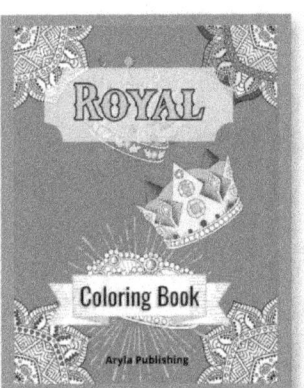

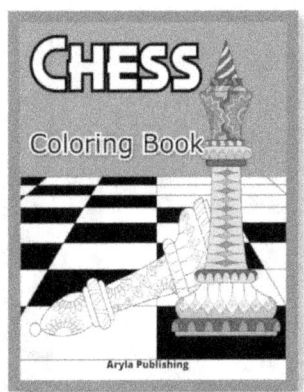

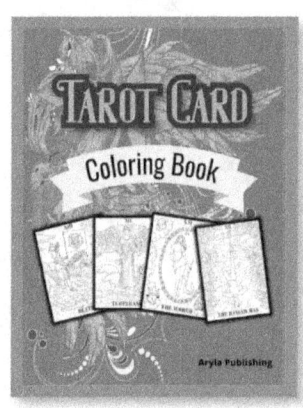

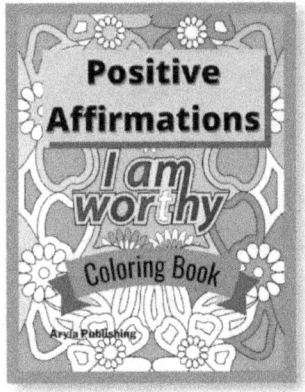

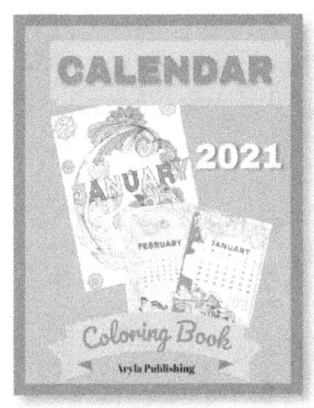

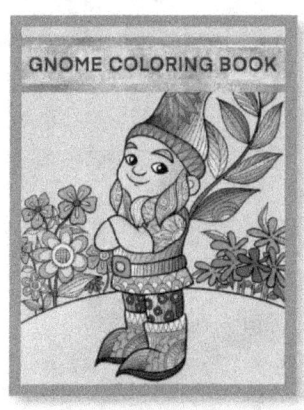

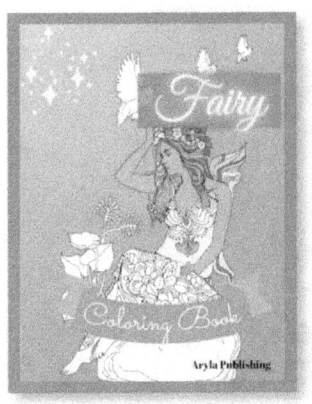

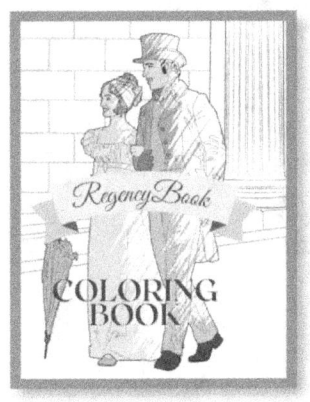

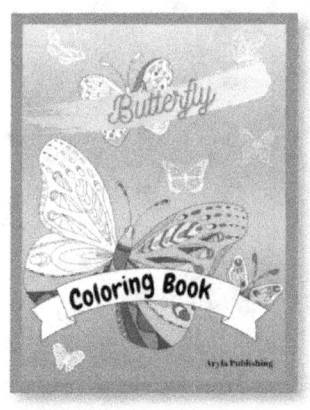

Color In Fun
Kids Books

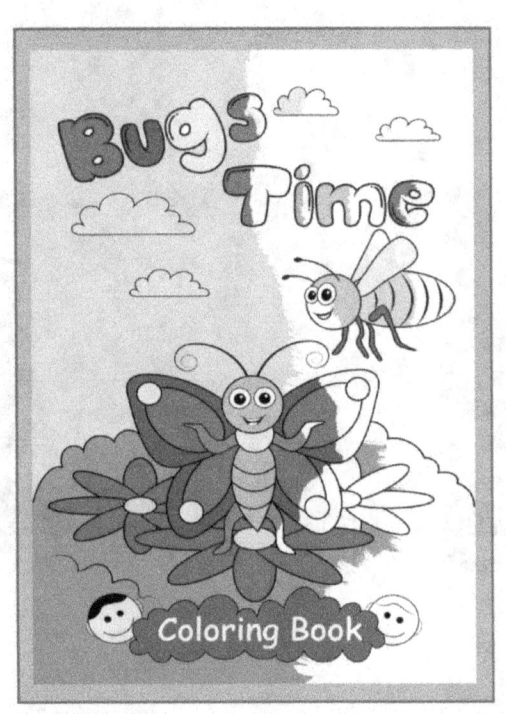

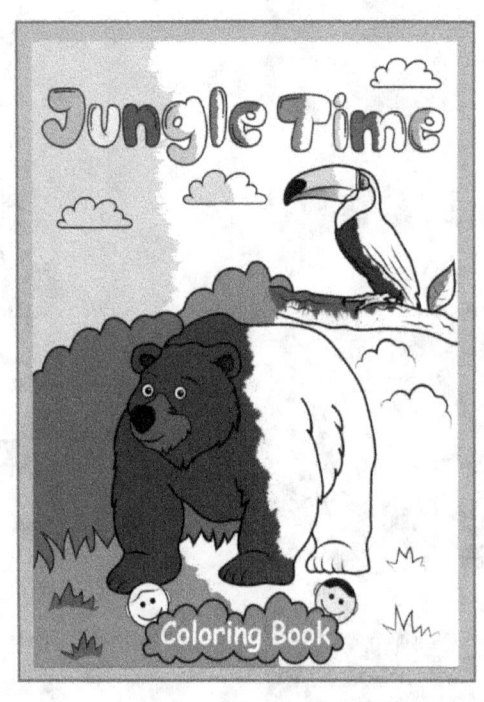

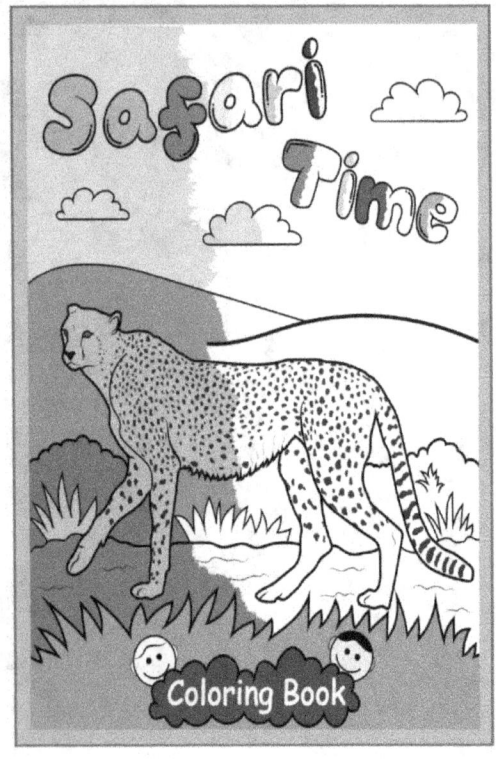

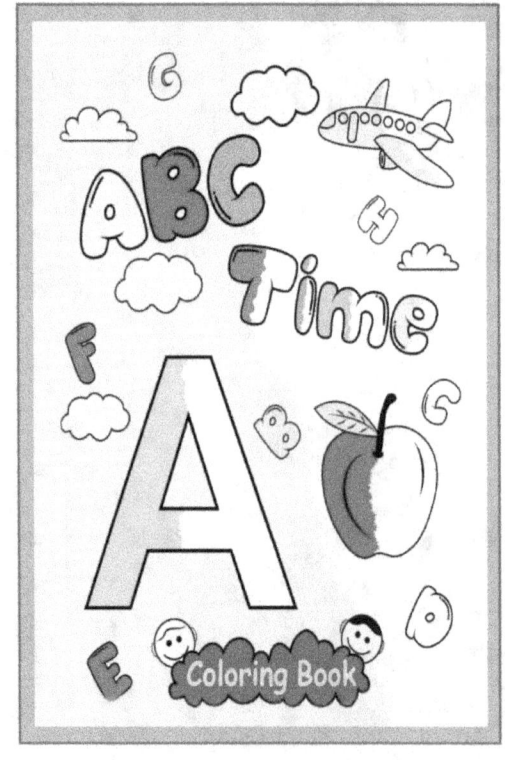

Visit **www.ArylaPublishing.com**

to find out about all new releases.

Follow us @arylapublishing on Twitter Instagram & Facebook

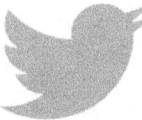  

Search for Aryla Publishing on

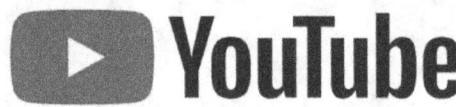

Check out our <u>Book Trailers</u>

<u>Subscribe</u> to keep up to date with new releases!

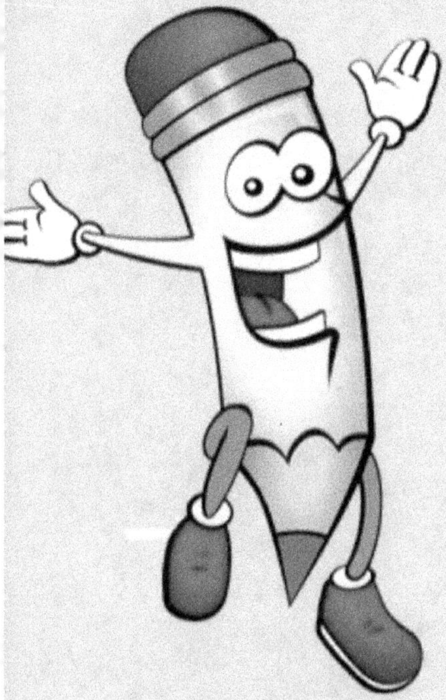

WE WOULD LOVE YOUR FEEDBACK

PLEASE LEAVE REVIEW AT:-

https://bit.ly/reviewblackinventors

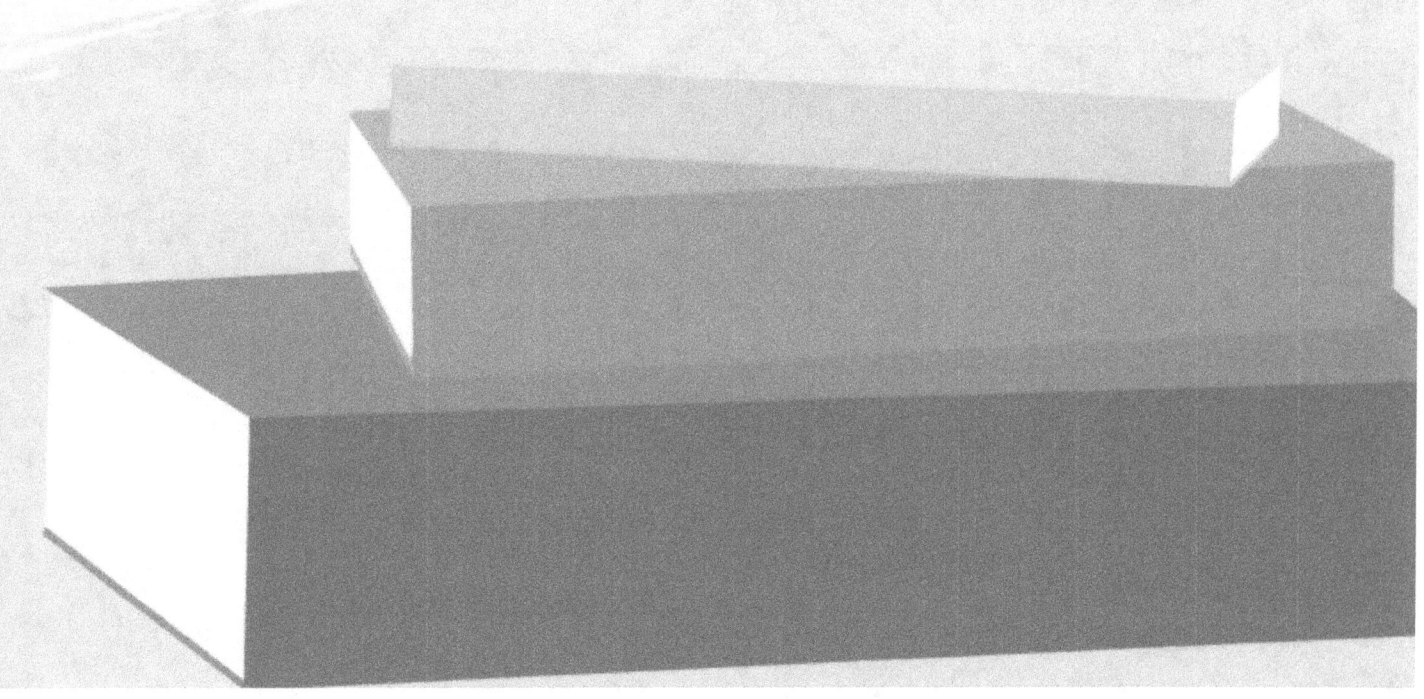

www.ingramcontent.com/pod-product-compliance
Lightning Source LLC
Chambersburg PA
CBHW081750220526

45468CB00008B/2310